Today

Smile

PHOTO BOX

THIS BOOK BELONGS TO

Hello

MY NAME IS

Copyright ©:
Unit for Expats and the Authors:
Maria Kofod Techow
Emilie Frijs Due
Bente Skovby Burke

Translation from Danish to English by:
Emilie Frijs Due og Jon Jay Neufeld

Editing by:
Maria Kofod Techow

Design by:
Camilla Engrob

Illustrations and photographs by:
Camilla Engrob

First edition published in Denmark by:

♡ **CENTER FOR FAMILIEUDVIKLING**

Unit for Expats
Center for Family Development
Østergade 5, 1
Copenhagen K
Denmark
www.familieudvikling.dk
mkt@familieudvikling.dk

This edition published in Great Britain by
Summertime Publishing.

ISBN: 978-1-915264-00-8

DEAR PARENTS!

You are probably asking yourselves a lot of questions concerning how your child feels about moving abroad, living in another country or moving back 'home'. The aim of this book is to guide children between the ages of 6 and 13 through the expatriation and repatriation processes, the book being divided into three parts: preparing to move ('Before you leave'), your time abroad ('While you are in the new country') and your return 'home' ('When you return to your passport country').

Young children will need your help working through the book. We hope that this can lead to meaningful conversations with your child about moving abroad. While older children can easily use the book on their own, we encourage you to invite them to share their thoughts and insights with you.

It's natural for parents to feel an urge to protect their children from the difficult feelings and challenges surrounding an international move. Consequently, they tend to focus only on the positive aspects. However, children are highly capable of dealing with the mixed feelings that they might experience during this process. Children need their parents to ask them about the thoughts and feelings that inevitably arise. That way they can find comfort in sharing them with those they are close to.

The book is full of advice for your child on how to adapt and maintain strong relationships and thrive. As parents, you can support your child in using these helpful strategies to cope with changes, make new friends and stay in touch with the people that stay behind once you move.

Enjoy the book and the enriching conversations with your child.

Safe travels!

Go

MY PERSONAL GUIDE
AND DIARY BEFORE,
DURING AND AFTER
MOVING ABROAD

A GUIDEBOOK FOR CHILDREN AGES 6 TO 13

"Come on!"
"Where?" said Pooh
"Anywhere",
said Christopher Robin
So they went off together
– Winnie the Pooh

Written by

MARIA TECHOW
EMILIE FRIJS DUE
BENTE SKOVBY BURKE
... AND NOW YOU TOO!

LAYOUT AND ILLUSTRATIONS BY
CAMILLA ENGROB

DEAR TRAVELLER

YOU HAVE BEEN GIVEN THIS BOOK BECAUSE YOU ARE MOVING ABROAD WITH YOUR PARENTS.
THE BOOK IS INTENDED TO HELP YOU PREPARE FOR SOME OF THE CHANGES THAT ARE ABOUT TO HAPPEN IN YOUR LIFE.

THE BOOK IS ALL YOURS, MEANING THAT YOU GET TO DECIDE IF OTHERS ARE ALLOWED TO PEEK OR IF IT'S ALL PRIVATE!
YOU WILL BE GUIDED THROUGH YOUR PREPARATIONS BEFORE YOU LEAVE, FIND SUPPORT WHILE YOU'RE ABROAD AND HAVE A HELPING HAND WHEN YOU GET BACK TO YOUR PASSPORT COUNTRY
THROUGHOUT THE BOOK YOU WILL FIND QUESTIONS AND PAGES TO FILL OUT.

THESE WILL HELP MAKE YOUR TIME IN YOUR NEW COUNTRY MORE FUN AND HELP YOU TO TREASURE ALL YOUR ADVENTURES. YOU WILL ALSO FIND SOME PAGES TO TEAR OUT, SMUDGE WITH DIRT, TAPE BITS AND PIECES TO OR JUST USE TO EXPRESS IF YOU'RE FEELING HAPPY OR SAD.

THIS BOOK IS YOUR SCRAPBOOK AND DIARY FOR YOUR MOVE ABROAD. YOU GET TO BE THE AUTHOR AND TELL YOUR OWN STORY!

THE BOOK HAS MANY QUESTIONS AND ACTIVITIES. YOU MIGHT FIND SOME OF THEM MORE FUN THAN OTHERS. YOU MIGHT EVEN FIND SOME OF THEM BORING – IF YOU DO, SKIP THEM AND MOVE ON TO SOMETHING ELSE. OR CHANGE THEM SO THEY MAKE MORE SENSE TO YOU. YOU CAN ALWAYS GO BACK AND FILL OUT SOME OF THE PAGES LATER. TAKE YOUR TIME!

In the back of the book you will find room for your friends and family to leave you a few words. If you want, you can ask someone who knows you well to write something in your book.

Passport country:
We will use this word throughout the book to describe the country where your passport is from – your 'home' country, which may not always feel like home.

The book has 3 parts:

1 BEFORE YOU LEAVE... LOOK FOR THIS SYMBOL

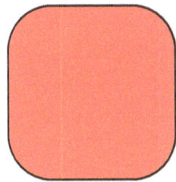

IN THE BOTTOM CORNER OF THE PAGE.
from page 8

2 WHILE YOU ARE IN THE NEW COUNTRY... LOOK FOR THIS SYMBOL

IN THE BOTTOM CORNER OF THE PAGE.
from page 46

3 WHEN YOU RETURN TO YOUR PASSPORT COUNTRY... LOOK FOR THIS SYMBOL

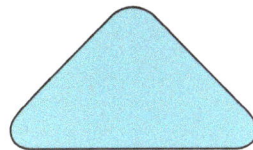

IN THE BOTTOM CORNER OF THE PAGE.
from page 126

YOUR PASSPORT COUNTRY

TCK

THE NEW COUNTRY

TCK

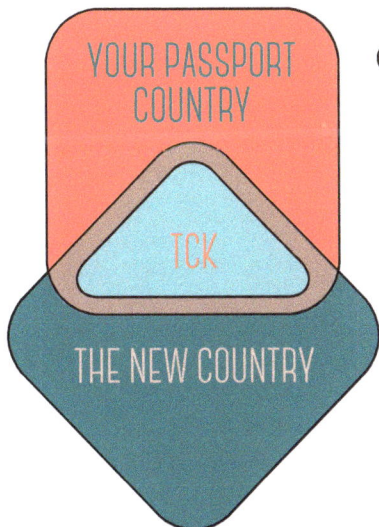

CHILDREN WHO MOVE ABROAD WITH THEIR PARENTS ARE SOMETIMES REFERRED TO AS THIRD CULTURE KIDS (TCKS), BECAUSE THEY GET TO EXPERIENCE THREE CULTURES. THE FIRST ONE IS THE CULTURE OF YOUR PASSPORT COUNTRY, THE COUNTRY YOU MIGHT BE LEAVING SOON. THE SECOND CULTURE IS THE CULTURE(S) YOU WILL BE LIVING IN FOR A PERIOD OF TIME. AND THE THIRD CULTURE IS A SPECIAL CULTURE THAT YOU WILL SHARE WITH OTHERS LIKE YOU WHO HAVE ALSO MOVED AROUND. MORE ON THAT LATER!

SAFE TRAVELS!

HOW TO USE THIS BOOK !

Read it and get new ideas

Take it with you

Ask others to write in it

Use it as a diary

Tear out some pages and give them to someone

Collect things in it

Write down your thoughts

Use a pencil if you want to change stuff later

YOU MAKE UP THE REST!

But most importantly;

THIS BOOK IS ALLOWED TO GET DIRTY AND WORN.

Start right away!

BEFORE YOU LEAVE

WHILE YOU ARE PREPARING TO LEAVE, YOU PROBABLY HAVE A LOT ON YOUR MIND. ON THIS MAP, YOU WILL SEE A JOURNEY THROUGH SOME OF THE THINGS YOU MIGHT HAVE TO CONSIDER BEFORE LEAVING. YOUR JOURNEY MIGHT LOOK DIFFERENT THAN THE ONE ON THIS MAP. YOURS MIGHT GO IN DIFFERENT DIRECTIONS. FLICK THROUGH THE BOOK AND FIND THE MAP SYMBOL IN THE BOTTOM CORNER OF THE PAGE THAT BEST DESCRIBES WHAT YOU ARE GOING THROUGH.

START HERE

WHERE TO?

WITH WHOM AND WHAT?

itinerary

Saying Goodbye

ARRIVED

THOUGHTS AND FEELINGS

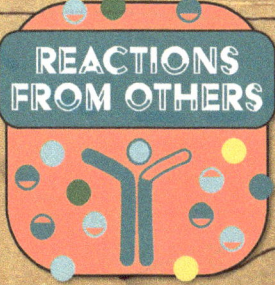

REACTIONS FROM OTHERS

THE WORLD IS YOUR playground!

MARK THIS

⊕ THIS IS WHERE I LIVE

♡ THIS IS WHERE THE REST OF MY FAMILY LIVES

✦ THIS IS WHERE MY FRIENDS LIVE

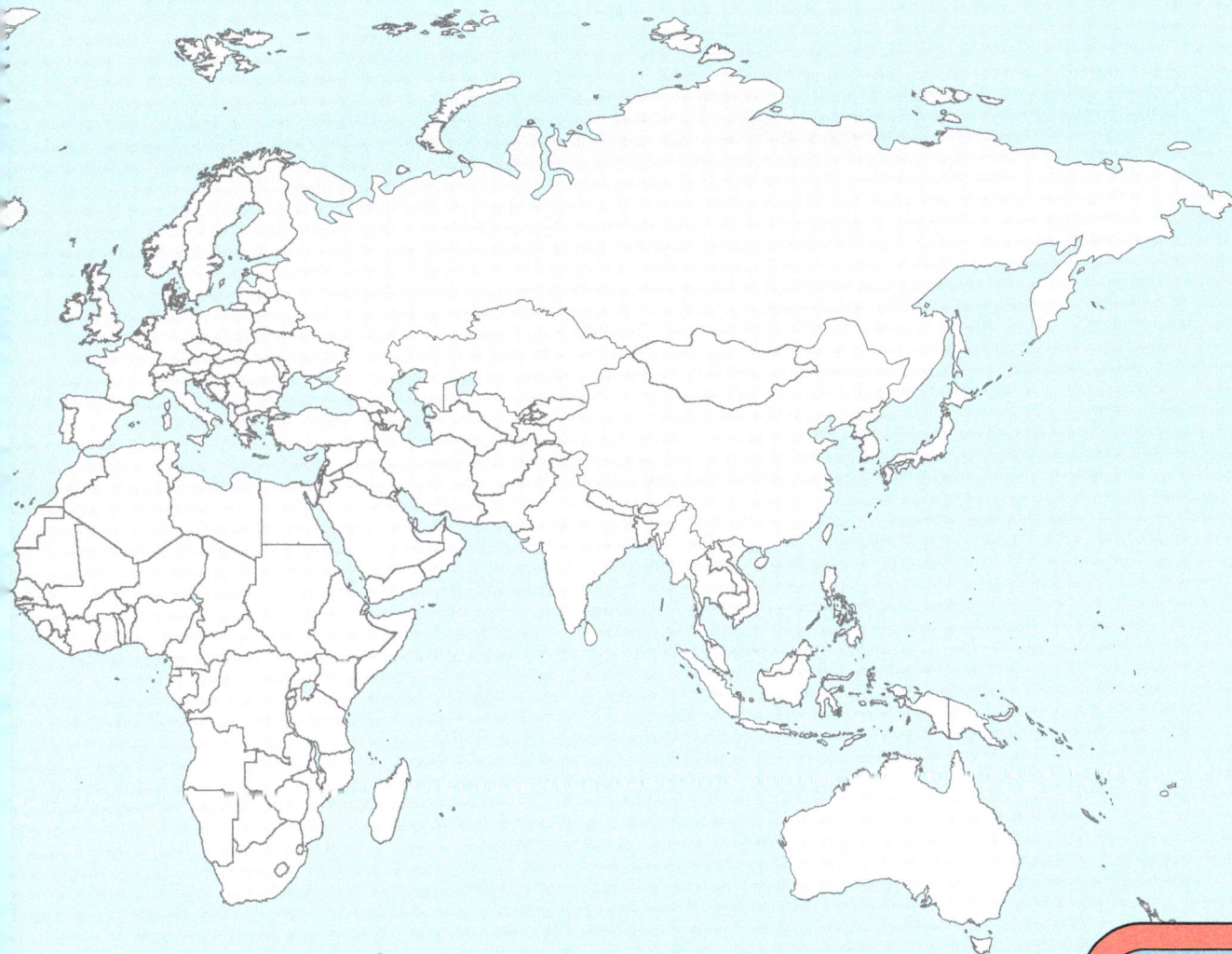

Colour the countries you have visited or lived in

Mark the country you are moving to

WHERE TO?

My Family

YOU

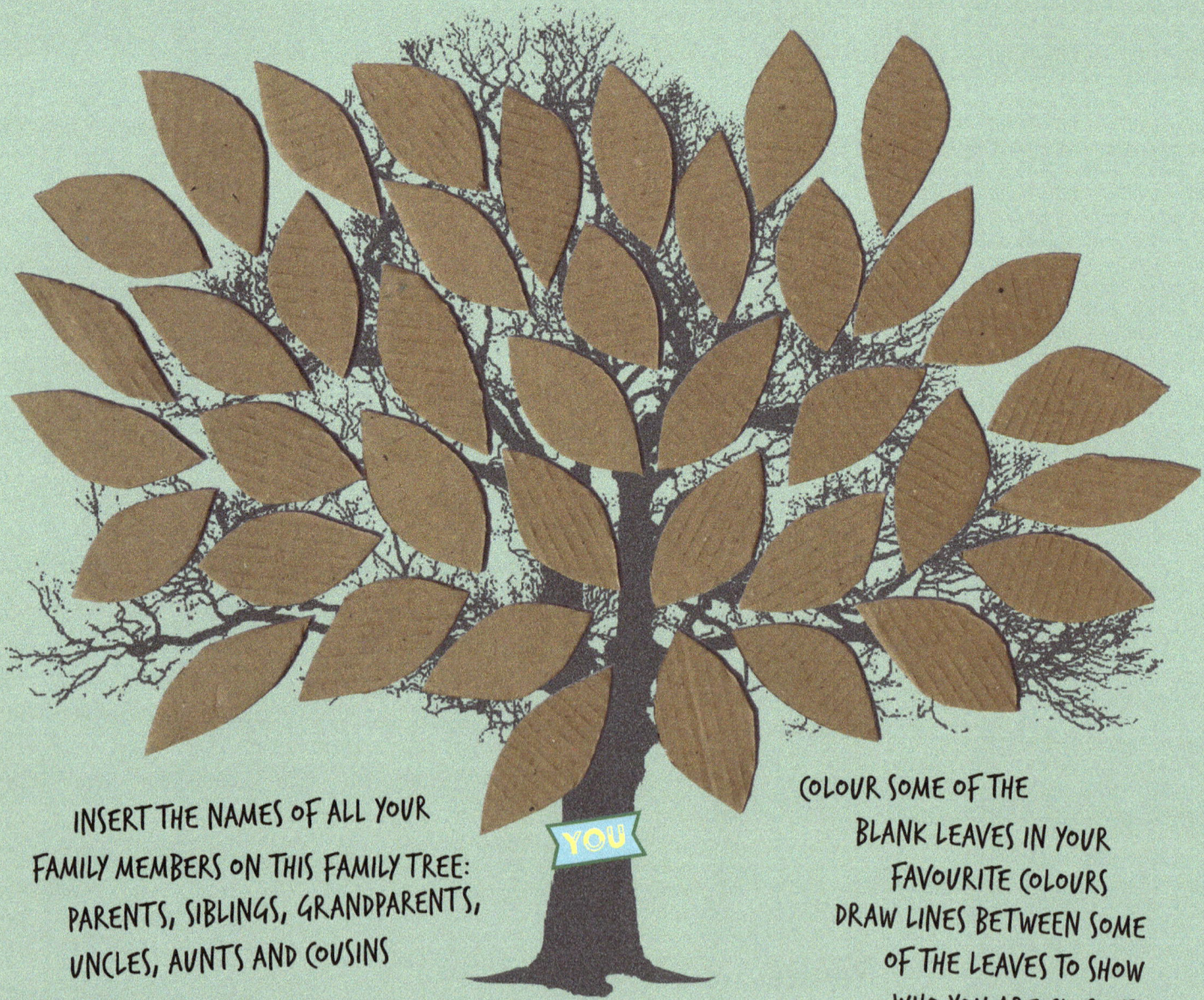

INSERT THE NAMES OF ALL YOUR
FAMILY MEMBERS ON THIS FAMILY TREE:
PARENTS, SIBLINGS, GRANDPARENTS,
UNCLES, AUNTS AND COUSINS

COLOUR SOME OF THE
BLANK LEAVES IN YOUR
FAVOURITE COLOURS
DRAW LINES BETWEEN SOME
OF THE LEAVES TO SHOW
WHO YOU ARE CLOSE TO

MORE ABOUT MY FAMILY
Who are we?

AGE

WEIRD HABITS

SIBLINGS

WORK

SCHOOL

FAVOURITE THINGS

WITH WHOM AND WHAT?

MORE ABOUT MY *family*

THINGS WE LIKE TO DO

THINGS I LIKE DOING WITH MY MUM

THINGS I LIKE DOING WITH MY DAD

THINGS I LIKE DOING WITH MY SIBLINGS

THINGS WE'RE GOOD AT

THINGS WE'RE NOT VERY GOOD AT

WHEN SOMEONE IN THE FAMILY GETS ANGRY OR STRESSED OUT, THEY

THE BEST TIME IS WHEN WE

OUR SPECIAL FEATURE AS A FAMILY IS

OTHERS WOULD DESCRIBE US AS

MORE STUFF ABOUT US

Keep asking until you run out of questions!

What will mum/dad be doing?

Who will I play with?

WHERE WILL I GO TO SCHOOL?

Will there be children my age?

Will it be dangerous?

Where am I going?

Why are we leaving?

How often will we go back to our passport country?

How will I make new friends?

What if something happens to us?

What does the moon look like there?

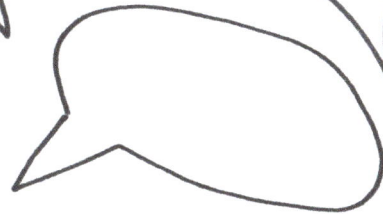

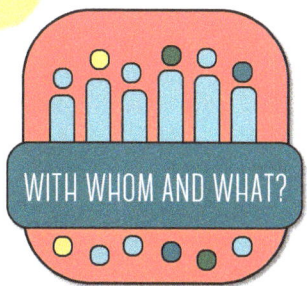

the EXPERT says

WITH ALL OF THE CHANGES GOING ON, IT'S IMPORTANT THAT YOU ASK A LOT OF QUESTIONS. LETTING YOUR IMAGINATION RUN WILD SOMETIMES LEADS TO WORRYING. AND SOMETIMES YOUR IMAGINATION CAN BE WORSE THAN WHAT IS ACTUALLY GOING ON. THERE ARE NO WRONG OR SILLY QUESTIONS. ASK YOUR PARENTS ABOUT EVERYTHING THAT'S ON YOUR MIND ABOUT MOVING! ASK AWAY!

WITH WHOM AND WHAT?

HERE IS SOME MORE ROOM FOR
WRITING DOWN THOUGHTS, FEELINGS OR OTHER
QUESTIONS THAT ARE ON YOUR MIND!

Thoughts and feelings

Situation:

YOUR PARENTS TELL YOU THAT YOU'RE MOVING TO ANOTHER COUNTRY

Thoughts:

THOUGHTS POP INTO PEOPLE'S HEADS ALL THE TIME. EVERY TIME A THOUGHT COMES AND GOES,

A NEW ONE POPS UP. THOUGHTS ARE SOMETIMES ABOUT OTHERS, SOMETIMES

ABOUT OURSELVES. THOUGHTS CAN BE BOTH PLEASANT OR DIFFICULT. THOUGHTS ARE

OFTEN OUR WAY OF UNDERSTANDING WHAT'S GOING ON IN OUR LIVES. OUR THOUGHTS AFFECT HOW WE FEEL.

HERE ARE A FEW EXAMPLES OF THOUGHTS:
I DON'T WANT TO MOVE.

I HAVE TO PACK ALL MY

STUFF IN BOXES.
THIS IS GOING TO BE SO EXCITING!

FEELINGS DESCRIBE HOW PEOPLE FEEL. OUR FEELINGS ARE USUALLY AFFECTED BY WHAT WE THINK AND WHAT

WE'RE DOING. FEELINGS CAN BE PLEASANT, BUT THEY CAN ALSO BE DIFFICULT AND MAKE MOODS

CHANGE! SOMETIMES FEELINGS LAST A LONG TIME, SOMETIMES THEY DISAPPEAR QUICKLY. FEELINGS ARE OFTEN DESCRIBED

IN A SINGLE WORD. HERE ARE SOME EXAMPLES:
HAPPINESS, SADNESS, EXCITEMENT

THOUGHTS AND FEELINGS

the EXPERT says

WHEN WE EXPERIENCE THINGS, THEY AFFECT WHAT WE THINK AND FEEL. OUR FEELINGS CAN EVEN MAKE OUR BODIES REACT AND THEY INFLUENCE HOW WE ACT. WHAT WE FEEL, THINK, HOW OUR BODIES REACT AND WHAT WE DO ARE ALL CONNECTED — LIKE FOUR CORNERS OF A DIAMOND.

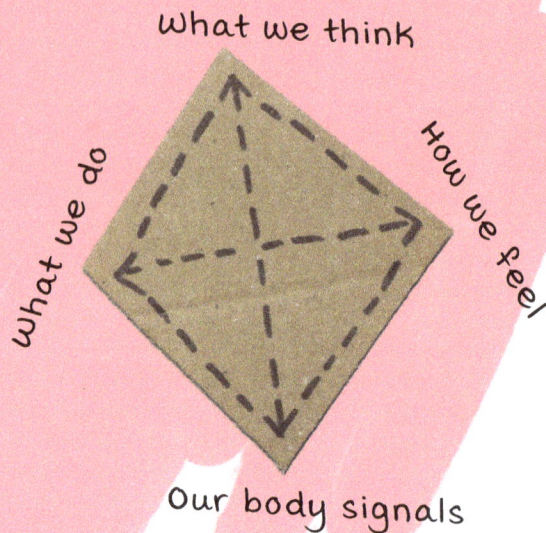

What we think

What we do

How we feel

Our body signals

Thoughts:
It's going to be exiting to get to do things that others don't

Feelings:
Happiness, Optimism

POSITIVE

Actions:
Search the Internet to learn more about the country

Body Signals:
Butterflies, fidgety

Thoughts:
I'm going to miss my friends. Will anybody want to play with me?

Feelings:
Sadness

NEGATIVE

Actions:
Staying in my room, distracting myself with my phone/tablet

Body signals:
Headache, stomach ache, unease

FILL OUT SOME MORE YOURSELF.

WHAT DID YOU THINK, FEEL, SENSE IN YOUR BODY AND DO WHEN YOU FOUND OUT THAT YOU WERE MOVING? POSITIVE THOUGHTS AND FEELINGS AND NEGATIVE THOUGHTS AND FEELINGS.

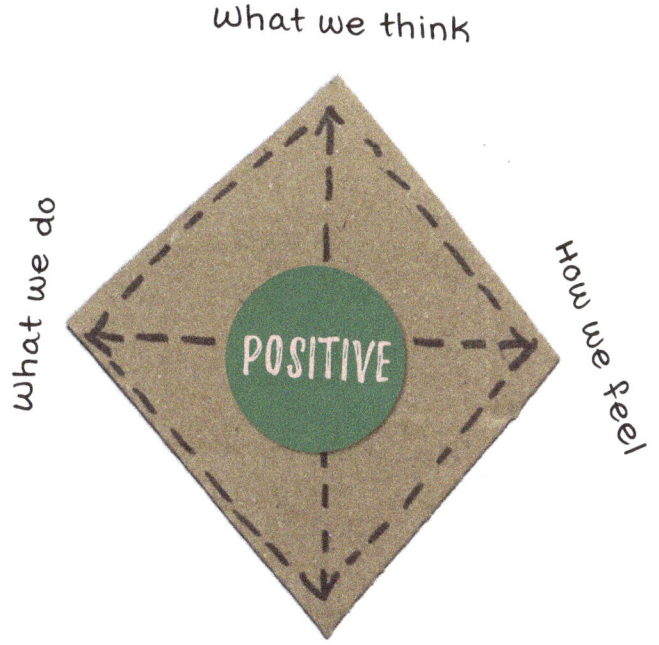

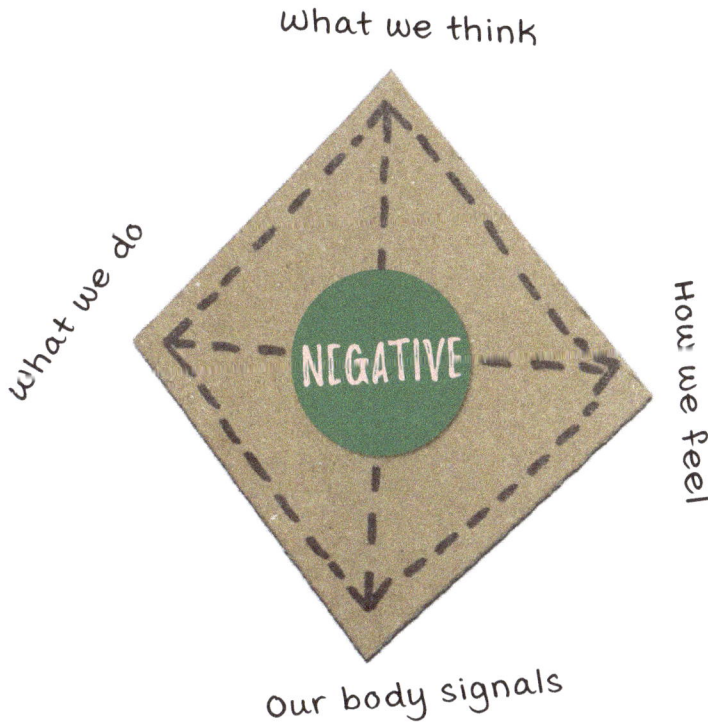

What we think

What we do

How we feel

POSITIVE

Our body signals

What we think

What we do

How we feel

NEGATIVE

Our body signals

THOUGHTS AND FEELINGS

These are our 6 most common feelings

SADNESS

JOY

DISGUST

ANGER

SURPRISE

FEAR

EXHAUSTED

CONFUSED

EXCITED

GUILTY

SUSPICIOUS

HYSTERICAL

FRUSTRATED

MALICIOUS

But there are lots of other feelings too. Which feelings did you experience when you found out you were moving?

FRIGHTENED

CAUTIOUS

DEPRESSED

FURIOUS

ASHAMED

SELF-SATISFIED

OVERWHELMED

OPTIMISTIC

LONELY

IN LOVE

JEALOUS

BORED

SATISFIED

EMBARRASSED

SHOCKED

SHY

ENVIOUS

AWKWARD

THOUGHTS AND FEELINGS

Have you ever
watched the film
Inside Out?

If not, watch it with your
family. It's about all the
feelings you can have when you
move somewhere far away!

TRY TO REMEMBER THE BODY SIGNALS AND FEELINGS YOU EXPERIENCED WHEN YOU FOUND OUT YOU WERE MOVING.

COLOURS

FEELING

- HAPPY ☐
- ANGRY ☐
- SURPRISED ☐
- SAD ☐
- DISGUSTED ☐
- AFRAID ☐
- ☐
- ☐
- ☐

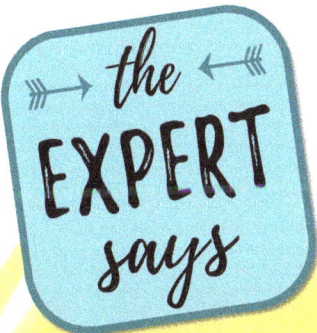

the EXPERT says

COLOURS SOMETIMES HELP US DESCRIBE OUR FEELINGS AND WHAT WE FEEL IN OUR BODIES

THOUGHTS AND FEELINGS

EVERYONE HAS AN OPINION

the EXPERT says

LOTS OF PEOPLE AROUND YOU MAY EXPRESS AN OPINION ABOUT WHAT IT'S LIKE TO HAVE TO MOVE ABROAD AS A FAMILY. SOME PEOPLE MIGHT THINK OF IT LIKE A LONG HOLIDAY. REMEMBER THAT YOU'RE NOT RESPONSIBLE FOR YOUR PARENTS' DECISION TO MOVE. LET THEM KNOW HOW YOU FEEL.

YOU MIGHT ALREADY HAVE NOTICED THAT A LOT OF PEOPLE HAVE OPINIONS ABOUT YOU AND YOUR FAMILY MOVING. SOME PEOPLE ASK QUESTIONS BECAUSE THEY REALLY CARE ABOUT YOU. OTHERS WILL GET SO EXITED AND CURIOUS THAT THEY WILL ASK YOU ALL SORTS OF QUESTIONS.

REMEMBER THAT YOU DON'T HAVE TO ANSWER ALL OF THE QUESTIONS THAT PEOPLE MAY ASK YOU. IF PEOPLE ASK YOU QUESTIONS YOU DON'T LIKE, HERE IS WHAT YOU CAN DO:

- CHANGE THE SUBJECT.

- ASK THEM HOW THEY WOULD FEEL: 'HOW WOULD YOU FEEL ABOUT HAVING TO MOVE?' OR 'WOULDN'T YOU MISS YOUR FRIENDS IF YOU WERE MOVING TO ANOTHER COUNTRY?'

- SAY: 'THANKS FOR ASKING ABOUT OUR MOVE, BUT I CAN'T ANSWER ALL YOUR QUESTIONS BECAUSE I DON'T KNOW THE ANSWERS MYSELF'.

- TURN AROUND AND LEAVE IF YOU GET UNCOMFORTABLE OR UPSET WITH THE QUESTIONS.

- TALK TO A FRIEND ABOUT IT.

ANNOYING REMARKS AND QUESTIONS

-YOU'RE SO LUCKY — YOU GET TO MOVE TO ANOTHER COUNTRY AND HAVE FUN!

-HOW ARE YOU GOING TO TALK TO PEOPLE WHEN YOU DON'T SPEAK THEIR LANGUAGE?

-ARE THERE LIONS AND TIGERS EVERYWHERE OVER THERE?

Have you gotten questions or remarks that made you annoyed, happy, frustrated or sad? What did you do about it?

_____

_____

_____

_____

_____

_____

_____

_____

REACTIONS FROM OTHERS

These pages are filled with advice for you before you leave from children who have also moved to other countries. If you can think of anyone you know who has moved abroad, ask them for their best advice and tell them what's on your mind!

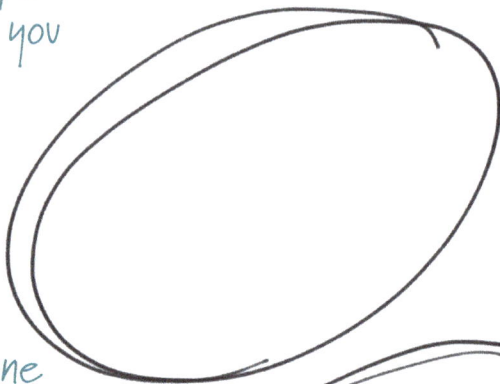

It helped me a lot that I stayed in touch with my old class in my passport country.
– Signe

Instead of withdrawing from your friends, let them know what you're going through!
–Anna

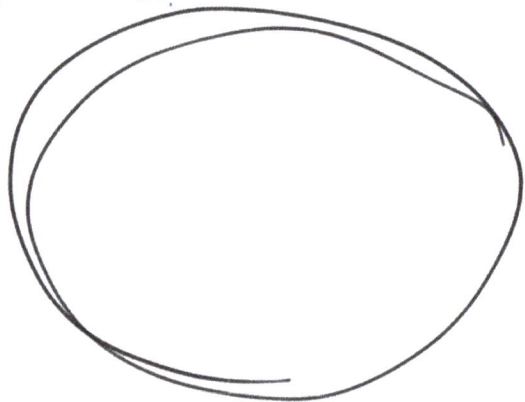

Make sure you bring a personal item with you from your passport country that reminds you of something nice.
– Simon

Stay in touch with your friends in your passport country. I lost some of mine because I forgot to do so. Also, gaming is a great way of relaxing.
– Ludvig

Remember to talk to your grandparents about how you want to stay in touch.
– Benjamin

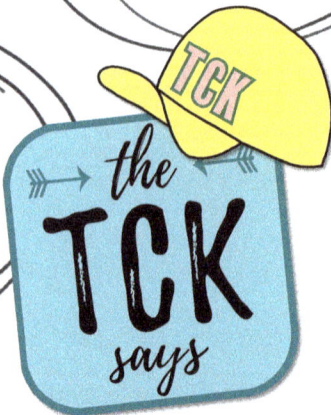

the TCK says

We said goodbye properly and my best friends helped me pack. I stayed in touch with my old friends back in my passport country, but I found new friends in Tanzania, so I sort of forgot about the old ones. I felt that my world was so different from theirs and that I didn't need my old friends in my new life.
– Ida

TCK

Missing my grandparents has been one of the hardest parts.
– Noah

TCK

TCK

Leaving my passport country wasn't that hard for me. I was so excited about my new life in Africa, so goodbyes were easy. I think I felt special because I was going to live in another country while everyone else was staying behind.
– Ida

It's funny how all of the toys we packed before leaving seemed uninteresting once we got there.
– Hannah

TCK

Saying Goodbye

the **EXPERT** says

BRINGING A FEW SIGNIFICANT PERSONAL THINGS WITH YOU WHEN YOU MOVE TO ANOTHER COUNTRY CAN BE IMPORTANT. BRING SOMETHING FROM YOUR OLD ROOM, YOUR FAVOURITE CUP, PICTURE OR TOY. THESE THINGS CAN HELP MAKE YOUR NEW HOUSE FEEL LIKE HOME.

Which things are you going to miss?

What would you like to take with you?

What's the difference between a house and a home?

SAYING GOODBYE
...or see you!

SAYING GOODBYE CAN BE HARDER FOR SOME PEOPLE THAN FOR OTHERS. JUST THE THOUGHT OF SAYING GOODBYE TO PEOPLE YOU CARE ABOUT — FRIENDS, CLASSMATES, PETS AND SO ON — CAN BE ENOUGH TO MAKE YOUR STOMACH ACHE! IT'S NORMAL TO FEEL THAT WAY EVEN THOUGH YOU MAY ALSO FEEL EXCITED ABOUT WHAT'S GOING TO HAPPEN. THESE FEELINGS CAN COME AND GO AND CHANGE FROM DAY TO DAY. ONE MOMENT YOU CAN FEEL HAPPY AND EXCITED AND THE NEXT MOMENT YOU'RE SAD AND JUST WANT TO CRY.

PREPARATION IS IMPORTANT WHEN MAJOR CHANGES ARE ABOUT TO HAPPEN IN YOUR LIFE.

LEAVING WELL IS ESSENTIAL. MAKE SURE YOU SAY GOODBYE OR 'SEE YOU'! MAKE PLANS FOR HOW TO STAY IN TOUCH AND HAVE A GOING-AWAY PARTY WITH THE PEOPLE WHO ARE IMPORTANT TO YOU.

Saying Goodbye

...to those who are important to me.

ON THE NEXT FEW PAGES, ASK YOUR GRANDPARENTS, AUNTS, UNCLES, COUSINS, FRIENDS OR SOMEONE ELSE WHO IS IMPORTANT TO YOU TO WRITE DOWN A FEW OF THE MEMORIES YOU SHARE.

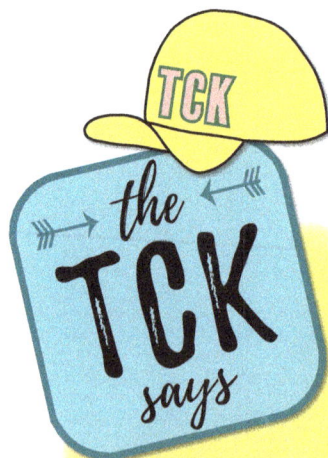

TCK

the TCK says

Best _____ ever

Catherine and her grandmother agreed to look at the same star as often as they could. That gave them lots of special starry nights together — even though they were apart.

Hello
MY NAME IS

Smile
PHOTO BOX

THE VERY FIRST THING I REMEMBER ABOUT YOU

THE FUNNIEST THING WE DID TOGETHER

OUR MOST PRECIOUS MEMORY

THIS IS HOW I THINK WE SHOULD STAY IN
TOUCH ONCE YOU MOVE ABROAD

I CAN'T WAIT FOR YOU TO
TELL ME ABOUT

WHERE TO

Hello
MY NAME IS

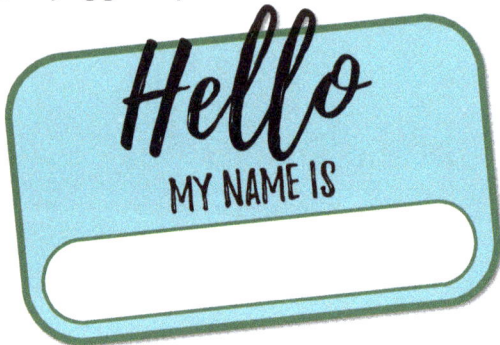

REMEMBER THAT TIME WHEN WE

_____
_____
_____

IT MEANT A LOT TO ME BECAUSE

_____
_____

I CAN'T WAIT TO
SKYPE/FACETIME/CALL YOU.
THE FIRST TIME WILL BE

_____
_____
_____
_____

Smile
PHOTO BOX

IF I GET TO VISIT YOU, I'D LOVE IT
IF YOU WOULD SHOW ME

_____
_____
_____

I'D LIKE YOU TO DRAW OR
SEND ME PICTURES OF

_____
_____
_____

WHERE TO

THE VERY FIRST THING I REMEMBER ABOUT YOU

_____

_____

_____

Hello

MY NAME IS

_____

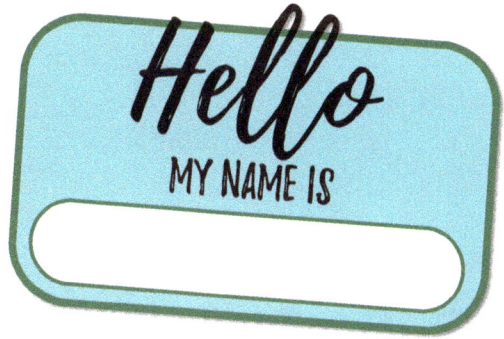

THE FUNNIEST THING WE DID TOGETHER

_____

OUR MOST PRECIOUS MEMORY

_____

THIS IS HOW I THINK WE SHOULD STAY IN
TOUCH AFTER YOU MOVE ABROAD

_____

_____

_____

_____

Smile

PHOTO BOX

I CAN'T WAIT FOR YOU
TO TELL ME ABOUT

WHERE TO

_____

_____

_____

I REMEMBER THE FIRST
TIME WE MET WHEN

_____

_____

_____

Hello
MY NAME IS

THE BEST GAME WE EVER PLAYED WAS _____

_____

_____

I'D LOVE FOR US TO STAY FRIENDS
EVEN THOUGH I WILL BE IN

_____

_____

_____

AND YOU WILL BE IN

_____

_____

_____

MAYBE WE CAN STAY IN TOUCH BY

_____

_____

_____

_____

_____

_____

Smile
PHOTO BOX

Best friends

I REMEMBER THE FIRST TIME
WE MET WAS WHEN _____
_____
_____

THE BEST GAME WE HAVE PLAYED WAS

_____

_____

_____

_____

_____

Smile
PHOTO BOX

I'D LOVE FOR US TO STAY FRIENDS
EVEN THOUGH I WILL BE IN

AND YOU WILL BE IN _____

_____

_____

_____

Best friends

Hello
MY NAME IS

MAYBE WE CAN STAY IN TOUCH BY

_____

_____

_____

Best friends

Hello
MY NAME IS

I REMEMBER THE FIRST
TIME WE MET WHEN

_____

THE BEST GAME WE HAVE PLAYED WAS

_____

_____

I'D LOVE FOR US TO STAY FRIENDS
EVEN THOUGH I WILL BE IN

_____

AND YOU WILL BE IN

_____

_____

_____

_____

_____

Smile
PHOTO BOX

MAYBE WE CAN STAY IN TOUCH BY

_____

_____

_____

_____

A little something from others I care about

STICK AN ENVELOPE TO THIS PAGE AND KEEP SOME
MEMORIES FROM THE LAST FEW DAYS BEFORE YOU MOVE

Saying Goodbye

OUR PLANS FOR THE LAST WEEK BEFORE WE LEAVE

TIME	SUNDAY	MONDAY	TUESDAY
7am–8am			
8am–9am			
9am–10am			
10am–11am			
11am–12am			
12am–1pm			
1pm–2pm			
2pm–3pm			
3pm–4pm			
4pm–5pm			
5pm–6pm			
6pm–7pm			
7pm–8pm			
8pm–9pm			

WEDNESDAY	THURSDAY	FRIDAY	SATURDAY

We are travelling from

Home

DO YOU KNOW YOUR ITINERARY ?

WE ARE LEAVING ON A

☐ SUNDAY ☐ MONDAY ☐ TUESDAY ☐ WEDNESDAY ☐ THURSDAY ☐ FRIDAY ☐ SATURDAY

AND WE WILL BE ARRIVING ON A

☐ SUNDAY ☐ MONDAY ☐ TUESDAY ☐ WEDNESDAY ☐ THURSDAY ☐ FRIDAY ☐ SATURDAY

WE LEAVE AT _____ O'CLOCK

AND WILL ARRIVE AT _____ O'CLOCK

READY SET GO

CAMERA

BOOKS I WANT TO READ

PAPER

THIS BOOK

EARPHONES

PHONE/TABLET

DECK OF CARDS

MY FAVOURITE CANDY

AUDIO BOOKS

WHERE TO

MUSIC

PENCIL AND
COLOURING PENCILS

GAMES

Our destination is

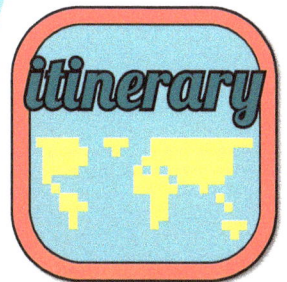

itinerary

WHO DID YOU SPEND YOUR LAST DAY WITH? WHO CAME TO THE AIRPORT WITH YOU?

WHAT ARE YOUR FAVOURITE
WAYS OF PASSING TIME
WHEN YOU'RE ON A PLANE
OR AT THE AIRPORT?

Here are some more ideas

Write the name of the country you're moving to, and write down all the words that come to mind.

Draw or write a story about your trip to show your friends.

Watch a movie on your tablet or if there is a screen on the plane.

Make up stories about the other passengers on the plane or at the airport. Imagine where they're going, where they come from and what their family is like.

Solve Sudokus.

Look out the window and try to guess what country you're flying over.

Write down everything you look forward to doing once you arrive.

itinerary

COLOUR OR DRAW SOME MORE

itinerary

YOU MADE IT!

A LOT OF EXCITING CHANGES AWAIT AND THERE WILL BE MANY THINGS TO FIGURE OUT. TO GUIDE YOU THROUGH ALL THAT, WE HAVE MADE A MAP OF THE ROUTE FOR YOU TO FOLLOW. CHANGE THE ORDER OF THE ROUTE IF YOURS LOOKS SLIGHTLY DIFFERENT THAN THIS ONE.

BE YOURSELF!

It's all new and exciting!

SETTLING IN TO EVERYDAY LIFE

EVERYTHING IS DIFFERENT AND STRANGE

START HERE

We have arrived in

This is what our new house looks like

THIS IS MY ROOM AND HOW I HAVE DECORATED IT

DRAW
IT LIKE
THIS

It's all new and exciting!

Go back and take a look at the diamond shape on page 18.
Write down what you were thinking, feeling, sensing in your body, and what you did.

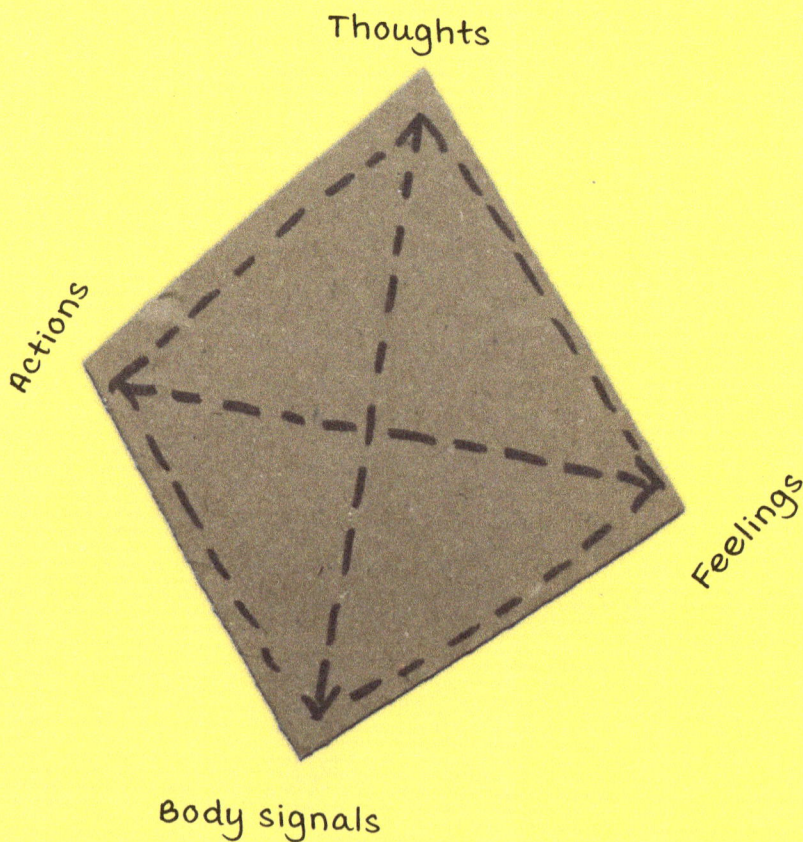

Thoughts

Actions

Feelings

Body signals

HERE IN ....
THEY SPEAK..................
HERE ARE SOME USEFUL
TRANSLATIONS

HELLO

SORRY

WHAT'S YOUR NAME?

PLEASE PASS ME

WELCOME

THANK YOU

DO YOU WANT TO PLAY WITH ME?

WOULD YOU PLEASE HELP ME?

WRITE DOWN SOME MORE
USEFUL PHRASES!

WHERE IS THE RESTROOM?

It's all new and exciting!

Embarrassing things I've said in another language or times when I didn't understand a word!

My little brother was having a hard time, mostly because of the language barrier. Once my brother asked why everyone said "ejneeer" when raising their hand. So I had to explain to him that they were saying "I know".
– Ida

TCK

Language is a big issue. You have to learn a whole new language!
– Ludvig

TCK

I once said Samaki (fish) instead of samahani (please)
– Ida

TCK

MAKING MISTAKES
CAN'T BE AVOIDED!

DON'T FORGET TO PRESS THE 'NEVER MIND'
BUTTON EVERY ONCE IN A WHILE!

It's better to make mistakes than to make nothing at all

Those who never make mistakes aren't living!

PRESS THE
BUTTON
AND MOVE ON!

NEVER
MIND!

It's all new and exciting!

MAKING MISTAKES
IS NORMAL
AND YOU LEARN
FROM THEM

WRITE DOWN SOME OF THE MISTAKES YOU'VE MADE

Tear off this side of the page when you're done.

WRITE DOWN WHAT
YOU WOULD LIKE
TO LEARN FROM
YOUR MISTAKES
OR DO DIFFERENTLY
NEXT TIME.

MAKE SENSE OF YOUR NEW COUNTRY!

Here are some ideas.
Write down some more.

Use your nose to smell all the new scents. Smell the air, the spices and the animals.

Use your hands and feet to touch your new surroundings. Touch the earth, the trees, the fruits and vegetables. Write letters or poems. Draw pictures or build a model of your surroundings. Dance and play sports!

Use your eyes to look around! Take in all the colours, shapes and buildings.

Use your eyes to read new books, watch videos and look at the people!

Use your mouth to taste the special local dishes! Sing new songs and talk to your new friends. Use your mouth to speak new words in a new language.

Use your ears to listen to a new language. Listen to new words, the sounds of nature, animals and local music.

It's all new and exciting!

WHAT DO THEY EAT HERE?

DRAW OR WRITE DOWN YOUR NEW FAVOURITE DISHES.

My favourite recipe

SHARE IT WITH
YOUR FRIENDS
AND FAMILY BACK
IN YOUR PASSPORT
COUNTRY!

It's all new and exciting!

CULTURAL DIFFERENCES

WHAT DO YOU KNOW ABOUT YOUR NEW COUNTRY BY NOW?
HOW DO PEOPLE GREET EACH OTHER?
IS IT HOT OR COLD HERE? MAYBE BOTH?
ARE THERE BEACHES, DESERTS OR MOUNTAINS?
WHAT KINDS OF ANIMALS LIVE HERE?

SOME THINGS MAY WORK THE SAME WAY THEY DO IN YOUR PASSPORT
COUNTRY — OTHER THINGS WILL PROBABLY BE VERY DIFFERENT.
THE COOLEST AND MOST INTERESTING THING
ABOUT LIVING IN ANOTHER COUNTRY IS FINDING
OUT HOW PEOPLE DO EVERYDAY STUFF IN
COMPLETELY DIFFERENT WAYS!

At first I was frightened by all the security guards everywhere. But you get used to it!
– Carl

TCK

On days where the Internet didn't work I almost went crazy!!
– Emily

TCK

SCARED

SURPRISED

SAD

WHEN VISITING A FRIEND, TEA AND BISCUITS MIGHT BE SERVED LATE IN THE AFTERNOON AND THEN DINNER AT 9PM! OR MAYBE THEY EAT DINNER AT 4PM AND THEN EVENING SNACKS.

YOU MAY FIND THAT WHEN VISITING A NEW FRIENDS' HOUSE EVERYONE LEAVES THEIR SHOES AT THE FRONT DOOR.

ALL BEGINNINGS ARE DIFFICULT

HERE ARE SOME EXAMPLES OF HOW DIFFERENTLY THINGS ARE DONE AROUND THE WORLD. HOW WOULD YOU FEEL IF ANY OF THIS HAPPENED TO YOU?

YOU MAY FIND THAT WHEN YOU'RE INVITED TO A BIRTHDAY PARTY BY SOMEONE IN YOUR CLASS, ALL THE PARENTS COME TOO! PEOPLE OF ALL AGES: BROTHERS, SISTERS, AUNTS AND UNCLES ALL JOIN THE PARTY AND HAVE FUN!

WHEN YOU GIVE A GIFT TO A FRIEND, THEY MIGHT SAY 'THANK YOU' — BUT WAIT TO OPEN IT UNTIL YOU HAVE LEFT.

MAYBE A FRIEND'S MOTHER WILL HAVE A BABY AND THE BABY WON'T HAVE A NAME FOR SEVERAL WEEKS. NO ONE WILL BE ALLOWED TO SEE THE BABY OR SEND GIFTS UNTIL THE BABY IS NAMED. WHEN THEY DO NAME IT, THEY HAVE A BIG PARTY, AND EVERYONE COMES TO WELCOME THE NEW BABY.

WHEN VISITING A FRIEND, THEY MIGHT GREET THEIR MOTHER BY KISSING HER ON BOTH CHEEKS AND MAYBE YOU WILL BE EXPECTED TO DO SO TOO.

WHEN ONE OF YOUR CLASSMATES MOVES AWAY, EVERYONE IN THE CLASS WILL BRAID A BRACELET FOR HER THAT SHE ISN'T ALLOWED TO TAKE OFF UNTIL IT FALLS OFF BY ITSELF.

FRUSTRATED

CONFUSED

HAPPY

EVERYTHING IS DIFFERENT AND STRANGE

SETTLING IN TO EVERYDAY LIFE

EVERYONE LEARNS HOW THINGS WORK IN THE COUNTRY WHERE THEY LIVE. WE LEARN THROUGH OUR PARENTS, FRIENDS, TEACHERS, FAMILY, SCHOOL, SPORTS CLUB OR CHURCH. WE LEARN WHO TO INVITE TO A BIRTHDAY PARTY, WHAT TO DO WITH A GIFT, AND WHEN TO EAT DINNER. MOST PEOPLE DO THINGS THE SAME WAY. THE HABITS AND CULTURE IN OUR COUNTRY COME FROM HISTORY, GEOGRAPHY AND WHAT WE BELIEVE TO BE RIGHT AND WRONG.

IN OTHER COUNTRIES, PEOPLE HAVE OTHER HABITS AND A DIFFERENT CULTURE, BECAUSE THEIR HISTORY, GEOGRAPHY AND RELIGION ARE DIFFERENT. THEY HAVE THEIR OWN IDEAS ABOUT WHAT'S RIGHT AND WRONG, GOOD OR BAD.

IF YOU'VE EVER GONE TO SCHOOL WITH SOMEONE FROM ANOTHER COUNTRY, YOU PROBABLY NOTICED HOW THEY TRIED TO FIT IN BY LEARNING HOW YOU AND THE REST OF THE CLASS DID THINGS. PERHAPS THEY LOOKED DIFFERENT, WORE DIFFERENT CLOTHES THAN THE REST OF YOU OR BROUGHT STRANGE THINGS TO SCHOOL. MAYBE THEY DIDN'T SPEAK THE LANGUAGE AS WELL AS THE REST OF YOU OR KNOW THE SAME GAMES AS YOU. MAYBE THEY ACTED LIKE THEY USED TO IN THEIR OLD COUNTRY AND YOU TRIED TO HELP THEM LEARN HOW TO 'FIT IN'.

NOW THAT YOU'RE THE ONE LIVING IN ANOTHER COUNTRY, YOU HAVE TO LEARN ABOUT THE COUNTRY'S CULTURE AND HABITS. THAT MAY NOT ALWAYS BE A LOT OF FUN. AND YOU MAY FEEL CONFUSED AND SILLY SOMETIMES FOR DOING STUFF DIFFERENTLY THAN EVERYONE ELSE. BUT ONCE YOU GET THE HANG OF IT, IT CAN BE FUN TO DO THINGS DIFFERENTLY! IT'S EXCITING TO LEARN THAT THE SAME THINGS CAN BE DONE IN LOTS OF WAYS AND THAT NO ONE WAY IS RIGHT OR WRONG. WHEN YOU MOVE BACK TO YOUR PASSPORT COUNTRY, YOU WILL HAVE LEARNED SO MANY COOL THINGS!

> IF ONE JUST KEEPS WALKING, EVERYTHING WILL BE ALL RIGHT
> – SØREN KIERKEGAARD

People do things differently in this country! Write down some of the new habits you have developed or ways you have started doing things differently than you used to.

SETTLING IN TO EVERYDAY LIFE

ANXIETY AND WORRY

FEELING ANXIOUS
Feeling nervous, fidgety or restless.

Shaking, muscles tighten up, breathing fast, stomach aches, sweating or freezing.

Losing control

IT'S COMPLETELY NORMAL TO GET ANXIOUS WHEN EXPERIENCING SOMETHING NEW AND UNFAMILIAR. ANXIETY IS A FEELING THAT IS OFTEN RELATED TO THE FUTURE

"What will happen?"

IT'S SOMETHING WE THINK WE AREN'T IN CONTROL OF
IT'S OVERESTIMATING DANGER
IT'S BELIEVING SOMETHING IS MUCH WORSE THAN IT ACTUALLY IS
OUR IMAGINATION IS OFTEN WORSE THAN REALITY
WE UNDERESTIMATE OURSELVES AND THINK THAT WE CAN'T HANDLE WHAT WE'RE AFRAID OF

"Things aren't going to work out"

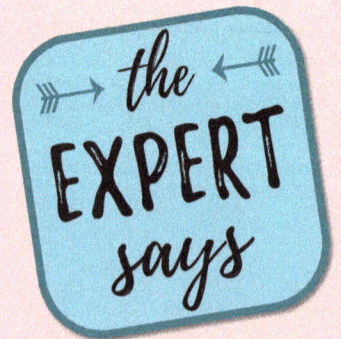

THE BEST WAY OF DEALING WITH ANXIETY IS BY FACING IT!
ONE WAY OF FACING IT IS BY NAMING YOUR FEARS:
I'M ANXIOUS THAT
_____

I'M AFRAID THAT
_____

the EXPERT says

TRY TO THINK OF OTHER WAYS OF HANDLING THE SITUATION
SLOWLY APPROACH WHAT YOU'RE AFRAID OF AND YOU WILL OFTEN FIND THAT IT'S NOT THAT DANGEROUS AND THAT YOU CAN MANAGE IT!

THE OPPOSITE OF ANXIETY IS
courage

ANXIETY — WHAT I AM/HAVE BEEN AFRAID OF

✗ I'm afraid of thunder.

✗

✗

COURAGE — HOW I DEAL WITH IT

✗ The last time there was a thunderstorm I watched the lightning and said to myself out loud that it was beautiful and that I was safe.

✗

✗

the EXPERT says

Breathe in ⟶

SOMETIMES IT HELPS TO BREATHE SLOWLY AND ALL THE WAY IN TO CALM YOURSELF DOWN. THAT'S CALLED BREATHING IN SQUARES. IT ALSO HELPS TO TELL YOURSELF THAT EVERYTHING IS GOING TO BE ALL RIGHT AND THAT YOU'RE NOT IN DANGER. YOU CAN MANAGE THIS, BECAUSE YOU HAVE MANAGED DIFFICULT THINGS BEFORE!

Hold your breath

Hold your breath

Breathe out

POSSIBLY SOME WORRYING OR ANXIETY

STEP OUT OF YOUR COMFORT ZONE!

Write down some of the habits that keep you from taking chances! Are there some comfortable habits you are going to have to leave behind when you go?

TO DARE IS TO LOSE ONE'S FOOTING MOMENTARILY. NOT TO DARE IS TO LOSE ONESELF.

— Søren Kierkegaard

They will still be there when you get back, if you need them.

Where the
magic
happens

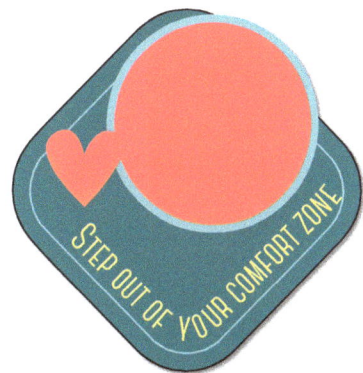

YOUR COMFORT ZONE

STEP OUT OF YOUR COMFORT ZONE

EIGHT TIPS FOR WHEN YOU FEEL HOMESICK
FROM JUDITH, 16

1. IT'S OKAY TO FEEL HOMESICK. YOU MIGHT FEEL HOMESICK BECAUSE YOU LOVE YOUR FAMILY AND FRIENDS SO MUCH THAT IT'S HARD TO BE AWAY FROM THEM. ALLOW YOURSELF TO MISS THEM AND BE SAD. DON'T FEEL ASHAMED OR THINK THAT MOVING HAS BEEN A FAILURE.

2. TAKE THINGS ONE DAY AT A TIME. TRY NOT TO THINK YOU HAVE TO MANAGE MONTHS AT A TIME.

3. NOTICE HOW HOMESICKNESS COMES AND GOES. RATE YOUR HOMESICKNESS WITH A NUMBER (1-10) AND NOTE HOW LONG IT TAKES BEFORE YOU FEEL A LITTLE BETTER.

4. TELL SOMEONE YOU'RE FEELING HOMESICK. FIND SOMEONE YOU CAN TALK TO IF IT GETS BAD. SHARE DIFFICULT THOUGHTS WITH OTHERS — THEN YOU'RE NOT ALONE.

5. WRITE TO YOUR FRIENDS AND FAMILY AND TELL THEM THAT YOU'RE FEELING HOMESICK. SHARE IT WITH THEM SO THEY KNOW HOW YOU FEEL. TELL YOUR FRIENDS THAT YOU NEED TO HEAR THAT THEY'RE DOING WELL, EVEN IF THEY MISS YOU, TOO.

6. STAY BUSY. BEING DISTRACTED IS SOMETIMES A GOOD WAY OF NOT LETTING YOUR THOUGHTS GET THE BETTER OF YOU!

7. MAKE THE TIME (30 MINUTES/WEEK) TO LOOK AT PICTURES OF THE PEOPLE YOU MISS — AND TRY TO DO SOMETHING ELSE IF YOU FEEL HOMESICK AT OTHER TIMES DURING THE WEEK.

8. TRY TO ENJOY WHERE YOU ARE AND HAVE FUN. IT DOESN'T HAVE TO BE A STRUGGLE ALL THE TIME. IT'S ALSO A UNIQUE TIME IN YOUR LIFE.

MY OWN ADVICE

_____

_____

_____

_____

_____

_____

_____

_____

_____

_____

_____

_____

_____

HOMESICK

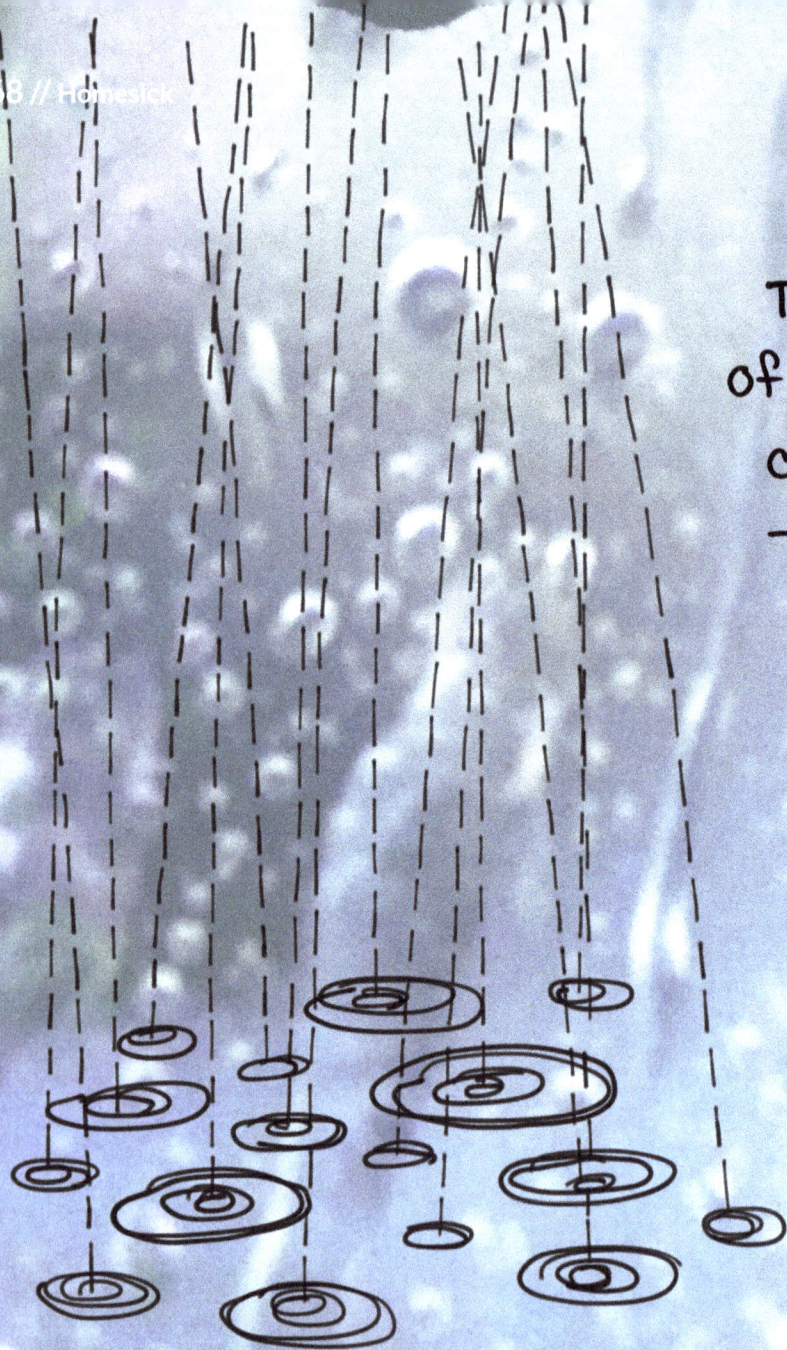

The ultimate place
of belonging and home
comes in relationships
– not places

Home is...

Home isn't a place, it's the people in it

Home is where
my family is

Home is where
you make it

These are the pieces of
life that can't be taken away
when they are built well, for
they are places of the heart

HOMESICK

Here is some space to write down all the nice things that others have said to you. Those words can be comforting to read if you're having a bad day.

What made
you feel
good today?

Write down
three things that
made your day today.

What are you
grateful for?

BE COURAGEOUS
AND EXPLORE THE
UNKNOWN

GETTING SETTLED IN TAKES TIME — THAT'S COMPLETELY NORMAL. KEEPING TRACK OF HOW YOU ARE

DOING EACH MONTH CAN HELP YOU SEE IF IT GETS BETTER. FOR SOME PEOPLE, SETTLING DOWN IS QUICK AND EASY. FOR OTHERS IT CAN TAKE ONE OR TWO YEARS, BUT IT GRADUALLY GETS BETTER. MARK THE MOOD THAT DESCRIBES EACH MONTH.

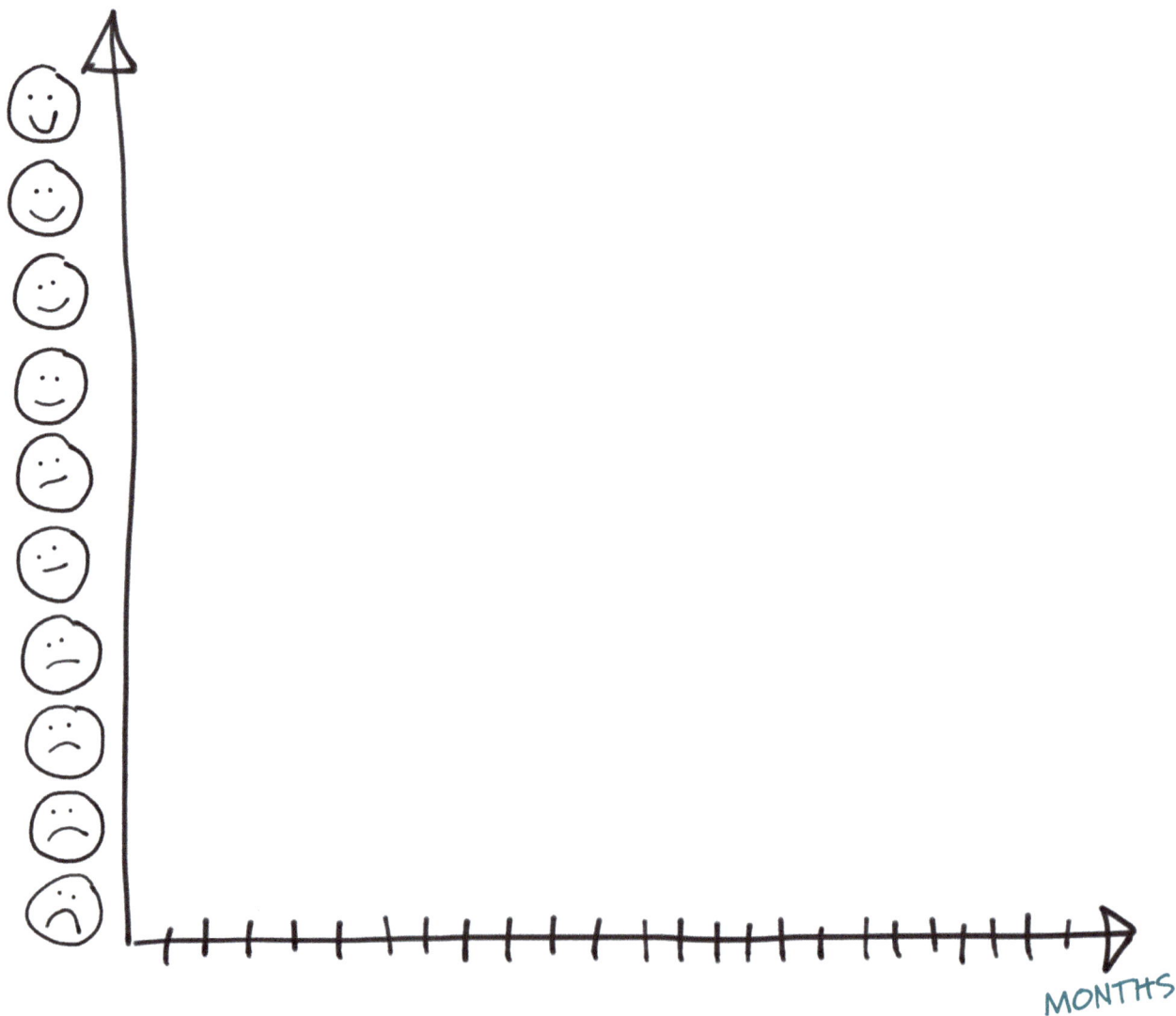

MONTHS

Never forget:

ONE OF THE BEST ASPECTS OF A TCK LIFESTYLE IS THE FUN IT CAN BE!

BE COURAGEOUS AND EXPLORE THE UNKNOWN

PLACES I WOULD LIKE TO VISIT WITH MY FAMILY

— Once you've been there, stick a souvenir or photo to this page

HAVING FUN IN MY LIFE

TRAVELLING AROUND, I HAVE SEEN SOME
FUN AND COOL PLACES IN MY LIFE:

ENJOY
THE JOURNEY

Here is some room for tickets, boarding passes, animal footprints, stains, spices, stamps, a pressed flower, photos or smells!
There is even room for a goat to lick the page!

PROOF THAT YOU WERE THERE
Collection pages

ENJOY THE JOURNEY

'Unpack your bags and plant your trees'
Lifelong advice from a father to his daughter

'Ruth, wherever you go in life, unpack your bags — physically and mentally — and plant your trees. Too many people never live in the now because they assume the time is too short to settle in. They don't plant trees because they expect to be gone before the trees bear fruit. But if you keep thinking about the next move, you'll never live fully where you are. When it's time to go, then it's time to go, but you won't have missed what this experience was about. If you never eat from the trees, someone else will' and he followed his advice by planting trees all around their home in Kano, Nigeria. Twelve years after going back to the United States, Ruth made her first trip back to Kano. As she picked and ate an orange off one of his trees, she knew her father had been right.

ENJOY THE JOURNEY

Words of wisdom

Ask someone to share their words of wisdom with you

the TCK says

The thing I like best about my life is living it

-Dirk

TCK

HOW TO MAKE NEW FRIENDS ?
Advice from TCKs

It might feel easier to just Skype with your old friends all the time. And it's fun and important — but going out and meeting new friends is also important!
–Camilla

It just happens! Maybe it's easier in international schools. Children there are so used to new faces arriving and others leaving. I made new friends quickly, even though I didn't speak the language. After-school activities and the playground were great ways!
– Ida

Joining a sports club or an after-school activity can be a good way.
–Thomas

IT'S NORMAL TO WORRY ABOUT MAKING FRIENDS. WE OFTEN TEND TO FORGET THAT WE'VE MET LOTS OF NEW PEOPLE BEFORE, BUT IT JUST TAKES TIME.
–JACOB

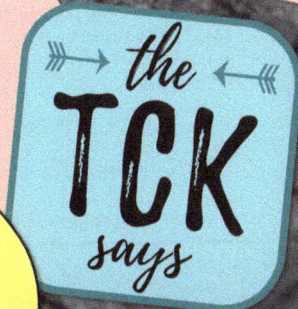

the TCK says

SHARE YOUR JOURNEY

Some days were annoying when we were in Tanzania. Like when you got teased or there was a power outage or homework was hard. But other days were more fun — where we went swimming or spent time with friends.
– Hannah

MORE ADVICE ON MAKING FRIENDS

- TAKE A WALK AROUND YOUR NEW NEIGHBOURHOOD WITH YOUR PARENTS AND FIND OUT IF ANY CHILDREN YOUR AGE LIVE NEARBY.
- GET YOUR PARENTS TO HELP YOU MAKE PLAY DATES WHERE YOU DO SOMETHING SPECIFIC THE FIRST FEW TIMES, LIKE SWIMMING, BAKING A CAKE OR PLAYING FOOTBALL TOGETHER.
- INVITE PEOPLE OVER FOR A WELCOME PARTY WHERE YOU CAN PLAY SOME GAMES.
- FIND OUT IF YOUR SCHOOL HAS MENTORS — WHERE SOME OF THE OLDER KIDS CAN HELP YOU SETTLE IN AT SCHOOL.

If you don't have any friends, you must try and talk to people anyway.
– Ingeborg

I use Facebook to keep up with my old friends. But it's important not to get stuck in the past if you want to make new friends.
– Ingeborg

- DRAW
- WRITE DOWN SOME NAMES
- ADD A PHOTO

How did you make your first friends?

Who would you like to be friends with?

What is your best advice on how to make friends?

Who are some of your new friends?

SHARE YOUR JOURNEY

On this page you can draw or colour with a new friend.
You can also ask one of your old friends back in your passport country to draw the same thing that you are drawing.

THE LITTLE PRINCE IS A BEAUTIFUL STORY – PART OF IT IS ABOUT MAKING FRIENDS AND HAVING TO SAY GOODBYE TO THEM.

It was then that the fox appeared.

"Good morning," said the fox.

"Good morning," the little prince responded politely, although when he turned around he saw nothing.

"I am right here", the voice said, "under the apple tree."

"Who are you?" asked the little prince, and added, "You are very pretty to look at."

"I am a fox," the fox said.

"Come and play with me," proposed the little prince.

"I am so unhappy."

"I cannot play with you", the fox said. "I am not tamed."

"Ah! Please excuse me," said the little prince. But, after some thought, he added:

"What does it mean— 'tame'?"

"You do not live here," said the fox. "What is it that you are looking for?"

"I am looking for men," said the little prince. "What does that mean — 'tame'?"

"Men," said the fox. "They have guns, and they hunt. It's very disturbing. They also raise chickens. These are their only interests. Are you looking for chickens?"

"No," said the little prince.

SHARE YOUR JOURNEY

"I am looking for
friends. What does that mean –'tame'?"
"It's an act too often neglected," said the fox. "It means to establish ties."
"'To establish ties'?"
"Just that," said the fox. "To me, you are still nothing more than a little boy who

is just like a hundred thousand other little boys. And I have no need of you. And you,
on you part, have no need of me. To you, I am nothing more than a fox like a hundred
thousand other foxes. But if you tame me, then we shall need each other. To me, you

will be unique in all the world. To you I shall be unique in all the world..."
"I am beginning to understand," said the little prince. "There is a flower.. I
think that she has tamed me..."
"It Is possible," said the fox. "On the Earth one sees all sorts of things."
"Oh, but this is not on the Earth!" said the little prince.
         The fox seemed perplexed, and very curious.
"On another planet?"
"Yes."
"Are there hunters on that planet?"

"No."
"Ah, that is interesting! Are there
chickens?"
"No."
"Nothing is perfect," sighed the fox.
But he came back to his idea.
"My life is very monotonous," he
said. "I hunt chickens; men hunt
me. All the chickens are just
alike, and all men are just alike.
And, in consequence, I am a little
bored. But if you tame me, it

will be as if the sun came to shine on my life.
I shall know the sound of a step that will be
different from all the others. Other steps send me
hurrying back underneath the ground. Yours will call
me, like music, out of my burrow. And then look: you
see the grain-fields down yonder? I do not eat
bread. Wheat is of no use to me. The wheat fields
have nothing to say to me. And that is sad. But you
have hair that is the colour of gold. Think how
wonderful that will be when you have tamed me!
The grain, which is also golden, will bring me back
to the thought of you. And I shall love to listen to the
wind in the wheat..."

The fox gazed at the little prince, for a long time.

"Please — tame me!" he said.

"I want to, very much," the little prince replied. "But I have not much time. I
have friends to discover, and a great many things to understand."

"One only understands the things that one tames," said the fox. "Men have no more time
to understand anything. They buy things all ready made in the shops. But there is no shop
anywhere where one can buy friendship, and so men have no friends anymore. If you want a
friend, tame me..."

"What must I do, to tame you?" asked the little prince.

"You must be very patient," replied the fox. "First you will sit down at
a little distance from me — like that — in the grass. I shall look at
you out of the corner of my eye, and you will say nothing. Words
are the source of misunderstandings. But you will sit a little
closer to me, every day..."

The next day the little prince came back.

"It would have been better to come back at the same hour,"

said the fox. "If, for example, you came at four o'clock in the afternoon, then at three o'clock I shall begin to be happy. I shall feel happier and happier as the hour advances. At four o'clock, I shall already be worrying and jumping about. I shall show you how happy I am! But if you come at just any time, I shall never know at what hour my heart is to be ready to greet you... One must observe the proper rites..."

"What is a rite?" asked the little prince.

"Those also are actions too often neglected," said the fox. "They are what make one day different from other days, one hour from other hours. There is a rite, for example, among my hunters. Every Thursday they dance with the village girls. So Thursday is a wonderful day for me! I can take a walk as far as the vineyards. But if the hunters danced at just any time, everyday would be like every other day, and I should never have any vacation at all."

So the little prince tamed the fox. And when the hour of his departure drew near—
"Ah," said the fox, "I shall cry."

"It is your own fault," said the little prince. "I never wished you any sort of harm; but you wanted me to tame you..."

"Yes, that is so," said the fox.

"But now you are going to cry!" Said the little prince.

"Yes, that is so," said the fox.

"Then it has done you no good at all!"

"It has done me good," said the fox, "because of the colour of the wheat fields." And then he added: "Go and look again at the roses. You will understand now that yours is unique in all the world. Then come back to say goodbye to me, and I will make you a present of a secret."

The little prince went away, to look again at the roses.

"You are not at all like my rose," he said. "As yet you are nothing. No one has tamed you, and you have tamed no one.

You are like my fox when I first knew him. He was only a fox like a hundred thousand other foxes. But I have made him my friend, and now he is unique in all the world."
And the roses were very much embarrassed.

"You are beautiful, but you are empty," he went on.

"One could not die for you. To be sure, an ordinary passer-by would think my rose looked just like you– the rose that belongs to me. But in herself alone she is more important than all the hundreds and thousands of you other roses: because it is she that I have watered; because it is she that I have put under the glass globe; because it is she that I have sheltered behind the screen; because it is for her that I have killed the caterpillars (except the two or three that we saved to become butterflies); because it is she that I have listened to, when she grumbled, or boasted, or even sometimes when she said nothing. Because she is my rose. "
And he went back to meet the fox.

"Goodbye," he said.

"Goodbye," said the fox. "And now here is my secret, a very simple secret: It is only with the heart that one can see rightly; what is essential is invisible to the eye."

"What is essential is invisible to the eye," the little prince repeated, so that he would be sure to remember.

"It is the time you have wasted for your rose that makes your rose so important."

"It is the time I have wasted for my rose–" said the little prince, so that he would be sure to remember.

"Men have forgotten this truth," said the fox. "But you must not forget it. You become responsible, forever, for what you have tamed. You are responsible for your rose..."

"I am responsible for my rose," the little prince repeated, so that he would be sure to remember.

SHARE YOUR JOURNEY

CLIQUES

FITTING IN AT SCHOOL

POPULAR

LONELY

NEW FRIENDS

DIARY PAGES
What's on your mind?

SHARE
YOUR
JOURNEY

These are some of the things that mean a lot to me and my family

SOMETHING WORTH FIGHTING FOR

SOMETHING THAT'S IMPORTANT TO ME

SOMETHING THAT I LIKE TO THINK OF

WHAT I BELIEVE IN

SOME OF THE VALUES THAT ARE IMPORTANT TO ME

SHARE YOUR JOURNEY

How we celebrate the holidays, decorate our Christmas tree and the names we call each other are just some of them - Ida

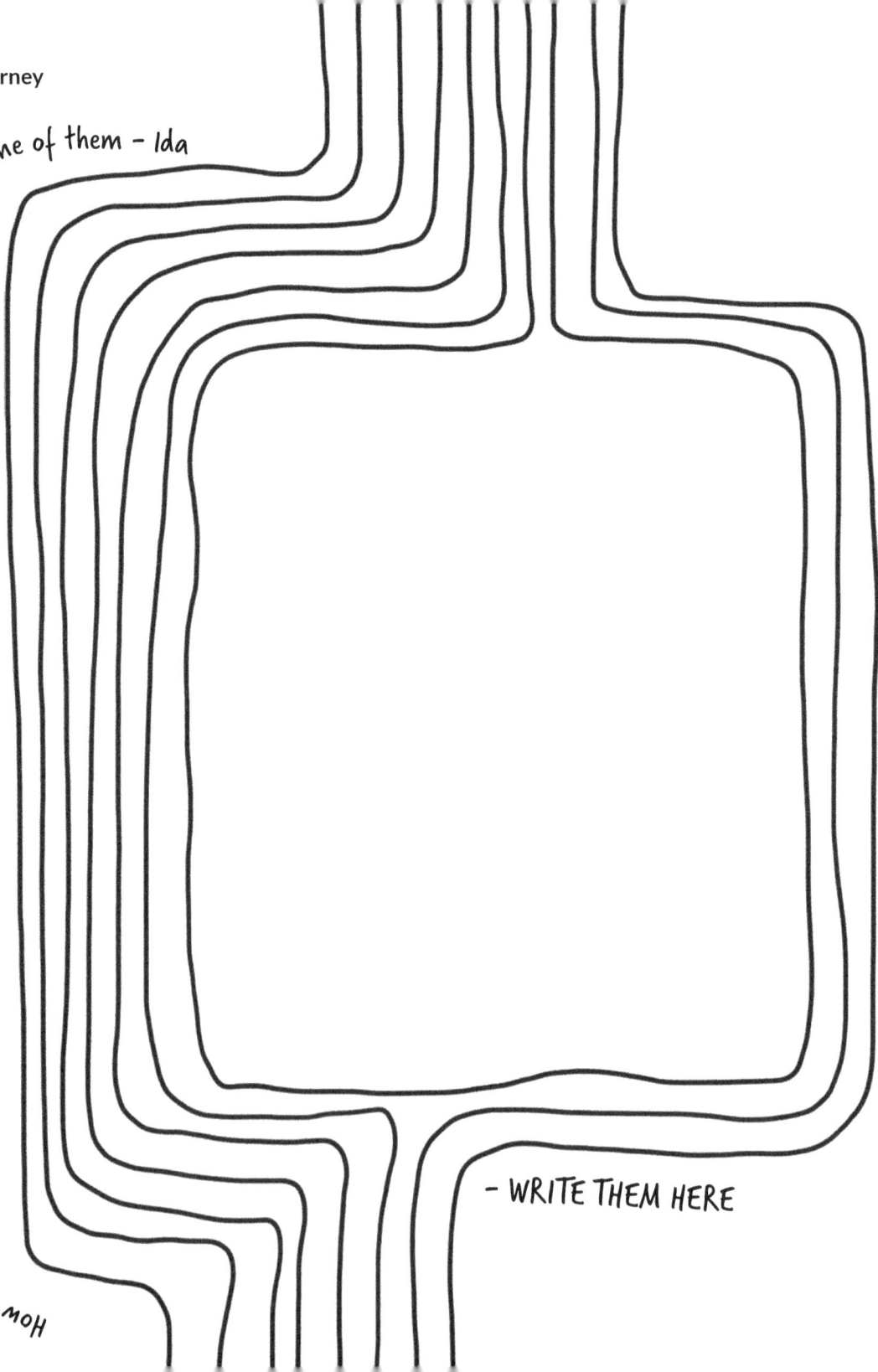

We have lots of traditions as a family from when we lived abroad.

- WRITE THEM HERE

FAMILY DIFFERENCES

ALTHOUGH YOU LEFT AS ONE FAMILY, YOU'RE ALL DIFFE-
RENT PEOPLE WITH YOUR OWN WAYS OF FACING THINGS.
IT'S COMPLETELY NORMAL THAT MOVING TO ANOTHER
COUNTRY IS A DIFFERENT EXPERIENCE FOR EACH OF YOU
OR THAT YOU FEEL DIFFERENTLY ABOUT IT.

SHARE
YOUR
JOURNEY

If you were to guess how the rest of your family feels about moving here, what would you say?

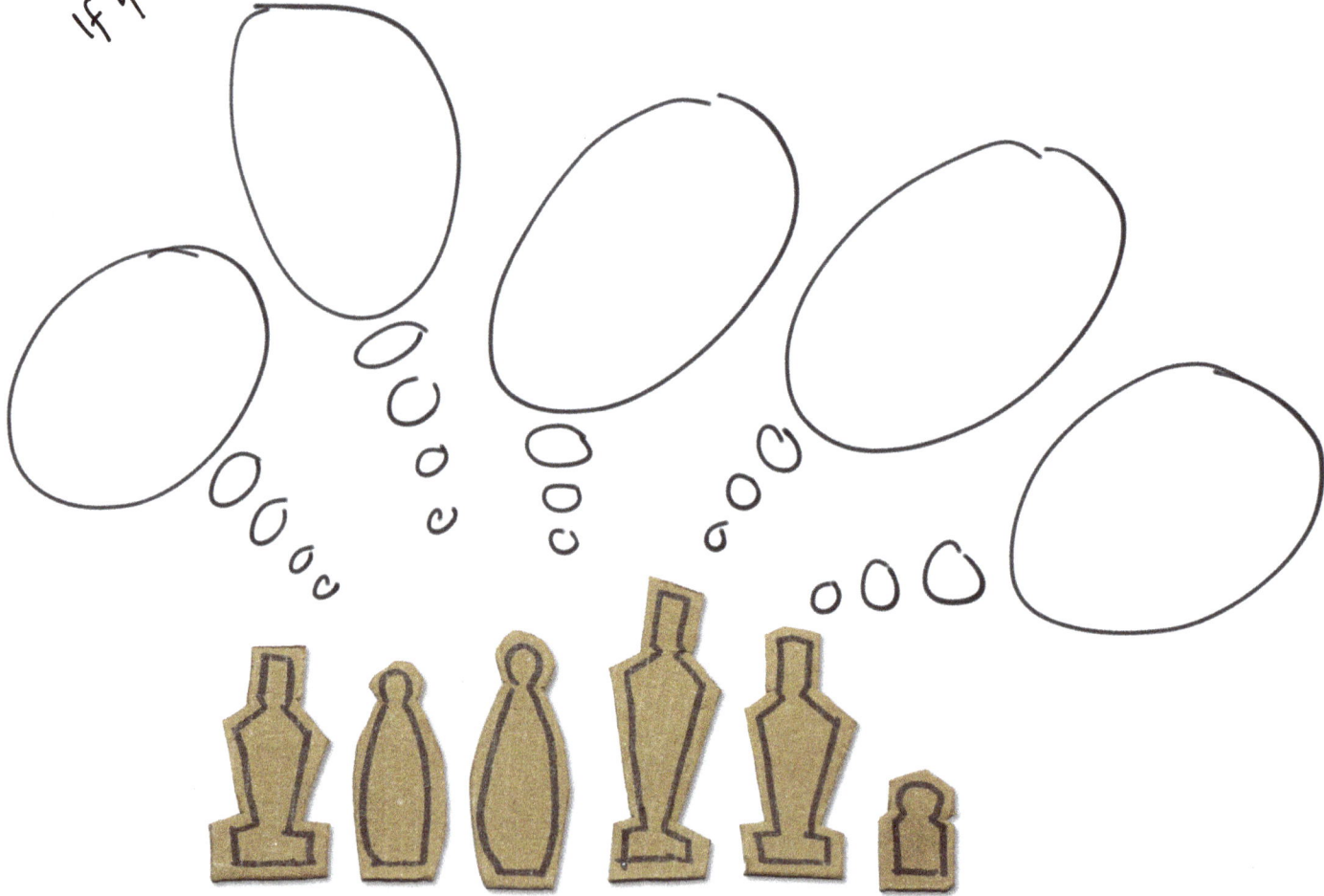

Have you talked about how you all feel?

In my family,
this is how we
help each
other out

SHARE
YOUR
JOURNEY

Write down their names, what they mean to you, and some of the stuff you've done together.

MY BONUS FAMILY

Sometimes when you move far away from your extended family you grow close to other people who live closer to you — your nanny, maid, teacher, neighbour or a volunteer in your community. These people can become bonus family members. Do you have any bonus family members?

WHO IS THERE FOR ME AND HAS ALWAYS BEEN THERE FOR ME? WRITE DOWN THEIR NAMES. THE CLOSER THEY ARE TO THE CENTER OF THE CIRCLE THE MORE IMPORTANT THEY ARE TO YOU.

ME

SHARE YOUR JOURNEY

Start here →

You have moved with your family — Yes →

You have moved abroad with your family — No → You're probably not a TCK – or maybe you've just forgotten

You have moved with your family — No ↓

You have moved abroad with your family — Yes ↓

You have been on an airplane — Yes → You're used to packing a suitcase

You have been on an airplane — No ↓

You're used to packing a suitcase — Yes ↓ You only like the food in your passport country

You're used to packing a suitcase — No → You've tasted all sorts of weird foods and dishes

You only speak one language — No → You only like the food in your passport country

You only speak one language — Yes ↓ You are used to hearing lots of different languages

You only like the food in your passport country — No → You've tasted all sorts of weird foods and dishes

You've tasted all sorts of weird foods and dishes — Yes →

You've tasted all sorts of weird foods and dishes — Yes ↓ You like most airports

You are used to hearing lots of different languages — Yes → You have a lot of stamps in your passport

You are used to hearing lots of different languages — No ↓

You have a lot of stamps in your passport — Yes ↓ You have a lot of stamps in your passport

You only like the food in your passport country — Yes ↓

You have a lot of stamps in your passport — Yes → You like most airports

You have a lot of stamps in your passport — No ↓ You're good at the geography of your passport country, but nowhere else

You like most airports — No → Yes → You might be a TCK who's not so fond of flying

You prefer hanging out with people who look and think like you — No → You're good at the geography of your passport country, but nowhere else

You prefer hanging out with people who look and think like you — Yes ↓

You're good at the geography of your passport country, but nowhere else — No ↓

You're good at the geography of your passport country, but nowhere else — Yes ↓ You like adventures

Your best friends are from your passport country — Yes → You like adventures

Your best friends are from your passport country — Yes ↓

You like adventures — No → You're probably not a TCK

You're probably not a TCK ← Yes

No ←

You have memories from several places around the world

— Yes → When telling stories, you often say 'and then we moved to...' — Yes → Home isn't really a place for you — it's something you share with people

Yes ↑

You know more about other countries than your passport country ← No ←

Yes ↑ Yes ↓

You love learning about new cultures — No → You could be a TCK — but one who doesn't like change

Yes ↓

You can calculate time differences quickly — No →

Yes ↓ (You're definitely a TCK! Welcome to the club. It's something very special)

You can calculate time differences quickly — Yes →

— Yes → You might not be a TCK — but just someone who's really good at languages and math

No →

Home isn't really a place for you — Yes ↓

Your accent changes depending on with who you're talking — Yes ↓

You have said a lot of goodbyes — Yes → You have memories from around the world

No ←

Yes / No →

You're more in touch with some of your friends online than in real life

Yes ↓

You have spent a lot of time with your siblings — Yes → You hesitate when answering the question 'where are you from?' — Yes → You have grown up in a different country than your parents

No →

No, I'm an only child ↘

Yes ↑ (You're definitely a TCK! Welcome to the club.)

Who am I?

SOME CHILDREN HAVE ONE CULTURE TO GROW UP IN, LIKE SOME OF YOUR FRIENDS BACK IN YOUR PASSPORT COUNTRY. OTHERS HAVE TWO CULTURES — LIKE IF ONE OF THEIR PARENTS IS FROM A DIFFERENT COUNTRY. BUT YOU ACTUALLY HAVE THREE CULTURES TO NAVIGATE IN:

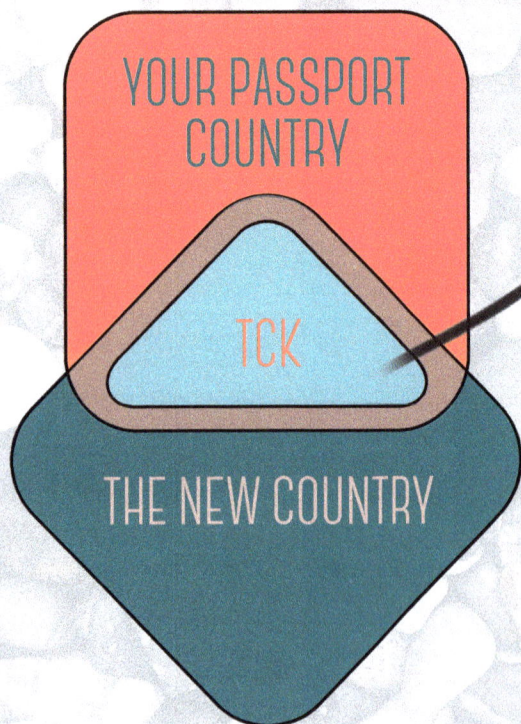

YOUR PASSPORT COUNTRY

TCK

THE NEW COUNTRY

A PARTICULAR CULTURE THAT OCCURS BETWEEN CULTURES. IT MAKES YOU UNDERSTAND AND RELATE TO OTHER CHILDREN WHO HAVE ALSO GROWN UP IN A DIFFERENT COUNTRY THAN JUST THEIR PASSPORT COUNTRY. THAT'S WHAT WE CALL BEING A 'THIRD CULTURE KID' (TCK).

GROWING UP A THIRD CULTURE KID MEANS A LOT OF THINGS.

It means finding out who you are as a person and what it means to be a TCK.

It means feeling connected and close to others and making friends with people who understand you.

It means feeling attached to more than one geographical place

It means taking one day at a time and enjoying the benefits despite the challenges.

It means having the freedom and courage to live a full life, wherever your feet are planted!

BE YOURSELF!

WHO AM I QUIZ

TICK OFF THE WORDS THAT BEST DESCRIBE YOU!

1

I AM:
- [ ] INTROVERTED
- [ ] EXTROVERTED
- [ ] SOCIAL
- [ ] QUIET
- [ ] NOISY
- [ ] CALM

2

I AM:
- [ ] FUNNY
- [ ] SHY
- [ ] SLOW
- [ ] FAST
- [ ] IMPULSIVE
- [ ] SENSIBLE
- [ ] ENERGETIC

3

I AM:
- [ ] THOROUGH
- [ ] SLOPPY
- [ ] PERFECTIONISTIC
- [ ] RELIABLE
- [ ] NEAT
- [ ] MESSY
- [ ] RELAXED

4

I AM:
- [ ] FRIENDLY
- [ ] WARM
- [ ] COOL
- [ ] KIND
- [ ] HELPFUL
- [ ] SUPPORTIVE
- [ ] CARING
- [ ] CONSIDERATE

5

I AM:
- [ ] THOUGHTFUL
- [ ] ANALYTICAL
- [ ] SPONTANEOUS
- [ ] SENSITIVE

RIP OUT THIS PAGE WHEN YOUR FRIEND HAS FILLED OUT THE QUIZ ON THE NEXT PAGE TO COMPARE YOUR ANSWERS. THERE IS NOTHING IMPORTANT ON THE BACK OF THE PAGE.

RIP OUT THIS PAGE TO COMPARE THE ANSWERS! THERE IS NOTHING IMPORTANT ON THE BACK OF THE PAGE

DO YOUR FRIENDS KNOW YOU?

GIVE THIS QUIZ TO A FRIEND FOR THEM TO ANSWER

1 THE OWNER OF THIS BOOK IS:
- ☐ INTROVERTED
- ☐ EXTROVERTED
- ☐ SOCIAL
- ☐ QUIET
- ☐ NOISY
- ☐ CALM

2 THE OWNER OF THIS BOOK IS:
- ☐ FUNNY
- ☐ SHY
- ☐ SLOW
- ☐ FAST
- ☐ IMPULSIVE
- ☐ SENSIBLE
- ☐ ENERGETIC

3 THE OWNER OF THIS BOOK IS:
- ☐ THOROUGH
- ☐ SLOPPY
- ☐ PERFECTIONISTIC
- ☐ RELIABLE
- ☐ NEAT
- ☐ MESSY
- ☐ RELAXED

4 THE OWNER OF THIS BOOK IS:
- ☐ FRIENDLY
- ☐ WARM
- ☐ COOL
- ☐ KIND
- ☐ HELPFUL
- ☐ SUPPORTIVE
- ☐ CARING
- ☐ CONSIDERATE

5 THE OWNER OF THIS BOOK IS:
- ☐ THOUGHTFUL
- ☐ ANALYTICAL
- ☐ SPONTANEOUS
- ☐ SENSITIVE

BE YOURSELF!

WHO AM I?

Write down everything that comes to mind

_____

_____

_____

_____

_____

_____

_____

_____

_____

_____

_____

_____

_____

_____

DON'T MIND IF YOU STAND OUT

IT'S OK TO BE DIFFERENT

Be proud of who you are and that you're not like everyone else

Don't walk in other people's footsteps — or you will never get ahead

The best page!

THE BEST GAME

THE BEST SUBJECT

THE BEST

THE BEST

THE BEST TEACHER

THE BEST FOOD

THE BEST

THE BEST

THE BEST

THE BEST SONG

THE BEST EXPERIENCE

THE BEST

THE BEST SMELL

BE YOURSELF!

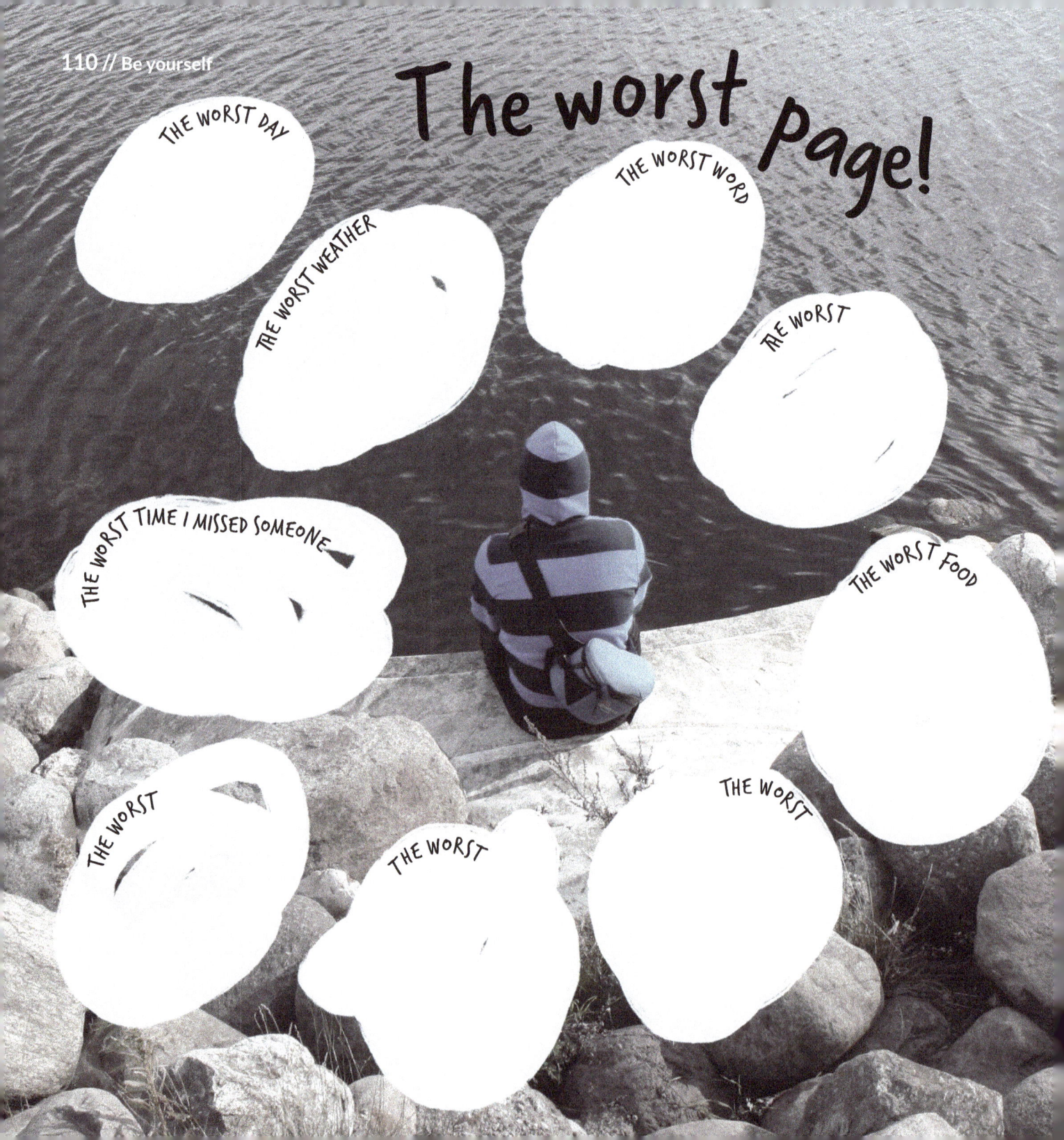

The worst page!

THE WORST DAY

THE WORST WORD

THE WORST WEATHER

THE WORST

THE WORST TIME I MISSED SOMEONE

THE WORST FOOD

THE WORST

THE WORST

THE WORST

THE UGLIEST

THE CUTEST

THE WEIRDEST

THE FUNNIEST

THE MOST DANGEROUS

THE SMARTEST

BE YOURSELF!

A page for missing

Missing friends and family is a sign that you love and care about them so much that being away from them is hard. Sometimes you may also miss things and places, traditions and specific memories. Allow yourself to miss things and be upset.
Don't be ashamed about it!
Describe who and what you miss:

What do you miss the most?

Who do you miss the most?

What helps you when you're missing someone or something?

When do you miss them/it the most?

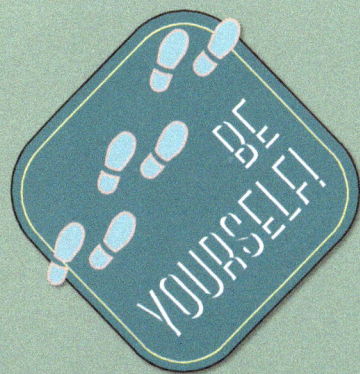

BE YOURSELF!

Sadness – feeling upset

SADNESS IS ONE OF OUR MOST COMMON FEELINGS. FEELING SAD, UPSET OR EVEN GRIEVING ONCE IN A WHILE IS NORMAL. WHEN YOU HAVE SOMEONE OR SOMETHING THAT YOU CARE ABOUT, THERE'S ALSO A FEAR OF LOSING THEM/IT OR THAT THEY/IT WILL DISAPPEAR. THAT DOESN'T MEAN THAT YOU SHOULD STOP CARING. LOVING AND CARING IS ALWAYS A RISK — BUT IT'S ABSOLUTELY WORTH IT!

FEELING SAD ABOUT SOMETHING IS A NORMAL REACTION TO AN UNUSUAL SITUATION.

'Sometimes it's nice to talk to my mum and dad about it. It also helps to Skype with my friends back home or play games with them.'

Advice from Elisabeth

'Don't focus on the things that aren't working out. Think about all the fun stuff — make a list of all the things that have worked out!'

From the film "inside out"

'Don't think too much about the knot in your stomach! Your new friends can help you untie that knot! Be an optimist.'

Advice from Ludvig

SOMETIMES PEOPLE TELL YOU TO PULL YOUR SELF TOGETHER AND MOVE ON. BUT REMEMBER THAT IT'S OKAY TO BE SAD.. IT CAN BE A GOOD IDEA TO DO SOMETHING THAT YOU KNOW CAN MAKE YOU FEEL BETTER.

WHEN YOU FEEL SAD, IT HELPS TO

- MOVE! GO FOR A WALK OR A RUN
- TALK TO SOMEONE
- LISTEN TO YOUR FAVOURITE MUSIC
- WATCH A FILM YOU LIKE
- WRITE DOWN THREE THINGS THAT YOU'RE GRATEFUL FOR
- WRITE DOWN WHAT MAKES YOU SAD — WHAT YOU FEEL, THINK AND DO
- ANY OTHER IDEAS?

Feeling sad:

CRYING

WANTING TO CRY OR FEELING THAT YOU
CAN'T STOP CRYING ONCE YOU'VE STARTED

HAVING A KNOT IN YOUR STOMACH

FEELING EMPTY

FEELING THAT THERE IS NOTHING NICE
TO LOOK FORWARD TO

the
EXPERT
says

BE
YOURSELF!

SAD

What made me sad?

What made me feel better?

MY PLAYLIST

The music that helps me when I feel sad or when I'm missing people or things

BE YOURSELF!

USE THIS CIRCLE AS A PIE CHART – DIVIDE THE CIRCLE INTO PIECES OF THE THINGS THAT MAKE YOU HAPPY AND GIVE YOU ENERGY

Joy

Joy is:

FEELING FULL OF ENERGY

BEING ENTHUSIASTIC

WANTING TO GIGGLE OR LAUGH

BEING HAPPY

FEELING YOUR FACE GLOW

FEELING BUTTERFLIES IN YOUR STOMACH

'We are going to have a good day, which will turn into a good week which will turn into a good month which will turn into a good year which will turn into a good life.'

From the film
INSIDE OUT

Joy

→ the ←
EXPERT
says

Friends, memories, days, animals, beauty, music or smells that made me happy

BE YOURSELF!

ANGER

ANGER IS A FEELING YOU CAN GET WHEN SOMETHING IS UNFAIR OR IF SOMEONE PREVENTS YOU FROM DOING SOMETHING. IF YOU ARE INTERRUPTED IN THE MIDDLE OF SOMETHING THAT'S IMPORTANT TO YOU OR IF SOMEONE OFFENDS YOU. ANGER IS A GOOD AND NORMAL REACTION. THE TROUBLE IS WHEN YOU GET ANGRY OVER SOMETHING THAT ISN'T UNFAIR OR WHEN YOU MISJUDGE WHAT WAS SAID OR DONE.

ANGER IS A FEELING THAT YOU CAN ACTUALLY DO SOMETHING ABOUT! BUT IT CAN BE REALLY HARD TO DO SOMETHING GOOD ABOUT YOUR ANGER IF YOU JUST WANT TO EXPLODE! SOMETIMES IT HELPS TO LET YOUR ANGER COOL OFF A BIT. GO FOR A WALK OR A RUN, MAKE ANGRY FACES, SHOUT, WRITE IT DOWN, USE A PUNCHING BAG OR TAKE A NAP.

WHEN YOUR ANGER HAS COOLED OFF A BIT, HERE ARE SOME WAYS TO MOVE ON:

1. TELL SOMEONE WHAT'S MAKING YOU ANGRY.

2. TRY DOING SOMETHING DIFFERENTLY. SOMETIMES THAT CAN CHANGE HOW YOU FEEL.

3. THINK DIFFERENTLY ABOUT THE INCIDENT THAT MADE YOU ANGRY. WHAT OTHER THOUGHTS COME TO MIND? WHAT WOULD YOUR BEST FRIEND DO IF THEY WERE IN YOUR SHOES?

→ the EXPERT ← says

Anger is:

FEELING LIKE YOU MIGHT FALL APART

FEELING LIKE YOU'RE LOSING CONTROL

WHEN YOUR WHOLE BODY STIFFENS, AND YOUR MUSCLES TIGHTEN UP

BARING YOUR TEETH

FEELING LIKE YOU'RE ABOUT TO EXPLODE

WANTING TO PUNCH OR THROW SOMETHING

MIND THE GAP

AAAaARGh
I'M FURIOUS!

ANGRY

SCRATCH THIS PAGE HARD WITH A PENCIL, RIP OFF THE PAGE ALTOGETHER AND CRUNCH IT INTO A BALL IF YOU'RE FEELING **ANGRY!**

BE YOURSELF!

ONE WAY

DEPT OF TRANSP

ONE WAY

DEPT OF TRANSPORTATION

Try this

It makes me so angry when I think of:

_____

_____

I start to feel:

_____

_____

My body reacts by:

_____

_____

Then what I end up doing is:

_____

_____

Instead, I could say:

_____

_____

To:

_____

_____

Instead of kicking, screaming and slamming the door, I could do something else like:

_____

_____

_____

Come to think of it, I might look at the situation differently. That way it makes me less angry and helps me understand that others:

_____

_____

_____

_____

BE YOURSELF!

DESCRIBE THE WORST TIME OF YOUR LIFE.

AND BE THERE FOR SOMEONE WHO IS GOING THROUGH SOMETHING SIMILAR RIGHT NOW.

Describe the best time of your life.

WRITE DOWN MEMORIES AND THOUGHTS ABOUT THAT TIME. SHARE THOSE THOUGHTS AND MEMORIES WITH SOMEONE YOU CARE ABOUT.

BE YOURSELF!

HOME?

REACHING THIS PART OF THE BOOK MEANS YOU'RE
PROBABLY ON YOUR WAY BACK TO YOUR PASSPORT
COUNTRY. YOU MAY FEEL AS THOUGH YOU'RE GOING HOME.
OR MAYBE YOU FEEL LIKE YOU'RE HEADED TOWARDS A
COMPLETELY NEW AND UNFAMILIAR PLACE, WHICH YOU ONLY KNOW
FROM A FEW HOLIDAYS. THERE CAN BE A LOT OF MIXED FEELINGS
ABOUT GOING BACK OR GOING TO YOUR PASSPORT COUNTRY. THIS PART OF
THE BOOK WILL GUIDE YOU THROUGH SOME OF THE TURBULENCE!

IF YOU'RE MOVING TO A NEW COUNTRY INSTEAD OF GOING BACK TO YOUR PASSPORT COUNTRY,
SOME OF THE PAGES FROM THE 'BEFORE' AND 'DURING' SECTIONS MAY ALSO BE HELPFUL.

WE HAVE MADE ANOTHER MAP OF THE ROUTE TO GUIDE YOU THROUGH ALL THIS.
CHANGE THE ORDER OF THE ROUTE IF YOURS LOOKS SLIGHTLY DIFFERENT THAN THIS ONE.

START HERE:

GOODBYE AGAIN

Special moments

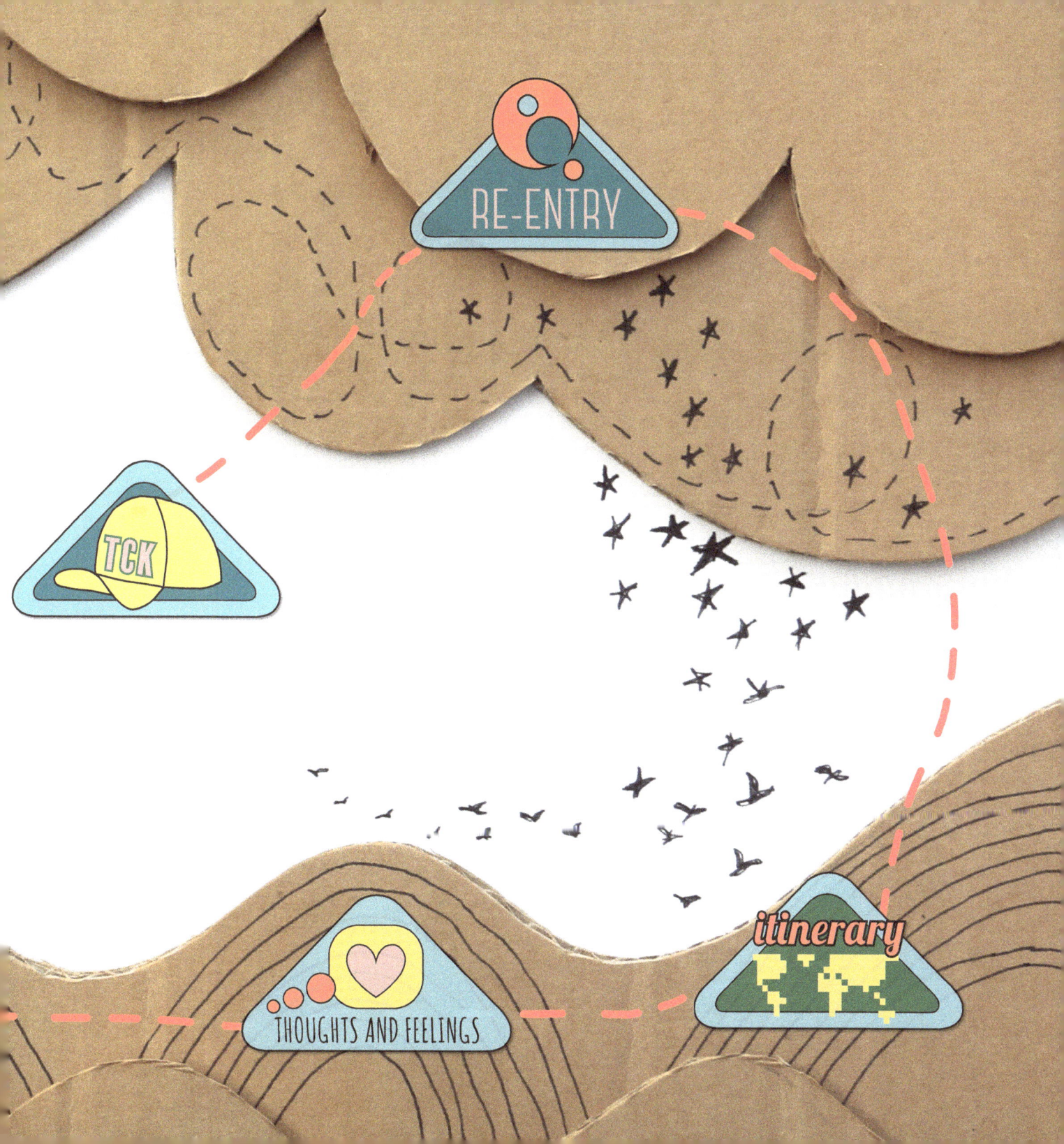

RE-ENTRY

TCK

THOUGHTS AND FEELINGS

itinerary

"For more
and more of us,
home has really less to
do with a piece of soil
than, you could say, with
a piece of soul."
Pico Iyer

WHAT I LOOK FORWARD TO THE MOST
ABOUT GOING BACK TO MY PASSPORT COUNTRY IS:

_____

_____

_____

_____

WHAT I DON'T LOOK FORWARD TO ABOUT
GOING BACK TO MY PASSPORT COUNTRY IS:

_____

_____

_____

_____

_____

_____

_____

GOODBYE AGAIN

Goodbye...again

You've done it before when you moved abroad and now it's time to do it again — to say goodbye!
You've probably gotten used to people coming and going and having to say goodbye. These next few pages will give you some time to think about what and who you will be saying goodbye to when you leave.

Who will you have to say 'goodbye' or 'see you later' to?

Who will it be hardest to say goodbye to?

Which places will you say goodbye to? Your house, school, local shop or football field etc?

MAKE SURE YOU SAY GOODBYE PROPERLY. SAYING GOODBYE TO PEOPLE YOU CARE ABOUT CAN BE HARD AND PAINFUL. DON'T FORGET THAT 'BYE' IS SOMETIMES ALSO 'SEE YOU AGAIN'.

the EXPERT says

Here is a poem about saying goodbye to your friends

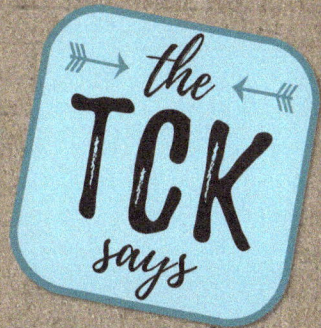

the
TCK
says

Signe, age 12,
wrote this poem for her friends after she moved
back to her passport country with her family.

HERE I STAND BEFORE A NEW LIFE AGAIN. I'M STANDING HERE,
I HAVE ALMOST LOST MY HOPE TO SEE THEM AGAIN SOMEDAY.
I HAVE, YES I HAVE, AND I DON'T KNOW HOW TO MAKE ME BE ME

I REMEMBER WHEN WE FIRST SAW IT AS EXTRAORDINARY.
YOU HAD ME MAKE A ROOM FOR ME, YOU MADE ME LOVE ME FOR ME.
AND HOW DID I PAY YOU BACK? I LEFT YOU, YES ITS TRUE.
I HAVE, YES I HAVE, AND I DON'T KNOW HOW TO MAKE ME BE ME.

'CAUSE WHEN I HOPE – IT LOSES FAST. IT BLOWS ME OUT, IT MAKES ME SAD.
I'M SO SO SORRY TO LEAVE YOU BEHIND IN MY PAST.
SO WHEN I SAID I WOULDN'T, IT MEANS I HAVE FALLEN TO MY DOOM.

I HAVE, YES I HAVE, AND I DON'T KNOW HOW TO MAKE ME BE ME.

GOODBYE AGAIN

GOODBYE TO PEOPLE YOU CARE ABOUT

SOME PEOPLE CHOOSE TO INVITE A FEW SPECIAL FRIENDS OVER TO SAY GOODBYE BEFORE THEY LEAVE. HOW WOULD YOU AND YOUR FAMILY FEEL ABOUT THAT? YOU DON'T HAVE

TO THROW A BIG PARTY. THE IMPORTANT THING IS SPENDING SOME TIME DOING SOMETHING YOU ENJOY TOGETHER WITH SOME OF THE PEOPLE YOU LIKE.

IS THERE ANYTHING IN PARTICULAR YOU'D LIKE TO SAY OR GIVE TO ANYONE BEFORE YOU LEAVE?

IS THERE SOMEONE YOU WANT TO SAY GOODBYE TO IN A SPECIFIC WAY?

'How lucky I am to have something that makes saying goodbye so hard.'

–Winnie the Pooh

Stay in touch

ON THE NEXT FEW PAGES YOUR BEST FRIENDS CAN WRITE DOWN A FEW THINGS FOR YOU BEFORE YOU GO BACK TO YOUR PASSPORT COUNTRY.

Moving back to my passport country was much harder than when we first moved away. Probably because I was older, and I had my friends and my boyfriend in Malawi. We spent a lot of time together before our departure and they came to the airport with us. Since then we've stayed in touch and kept up with each other's lives, gone to each other's weddings and so on!

– Ida

GOODBYE AGAIN

Hello

MY NAME IS

Smile

PHOTO BOX

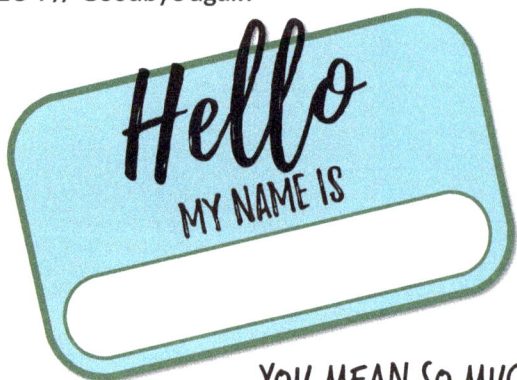

YOU MEAN SO MUCH TO ME BECAUSE

_____

_____

_____

_____

_____

I REMEMBER WHEN WE

_____

_____

THE BEST THING WE HAVE DONE TOGETHER IS

_____

_____

I'D LOVE TO STAY IN TOUCH WITH YOU, AND THE
BEST WAY FOR US TO DO SO IS:

_____

Best friends

WHERE TO

_____

_____

_____

Smile
PHOTO BOX

Hello
MY NAME IS

YOU ARE SO PRECIOUS TO ME BECAUSE

_____

_____

_____

_____

_____

I REMEMBER WHEN WE

_____

THE BEST THING WE HAVE DONE TOGETHER IS

_____

_____

_____

I'D LOVE TO STAY IN TOUCH WITH YOU,
AND THE BEST WAY FOR US TO DO SO IS:

_____

_____

_____

_____

Best friends

GOODBYE AGAIN

What would you like to bring with you to help you remember some of the stuff you've done in _____ ? Here you can insert pictures, tickets, candy wrappings, fabric, flowers or whatever helps you remember special moments. If you'd like to keep something that doesn't fit into the book, make a little 'memory box' to take with you. That way you can bring sand, stones, bones, old school assignments or other things that mean something special to you.

PROOF THAT YOU WERE THERE

Collection pages

Special moments

My special memories

What are your favourite
memories and moments?
Who did you share them with?
Draw them, write about
them, or show them on
these pages!

Special moments

my pets

Here are some of
the pets I have had
– stick a photo of them on this page.

Will we have pets back in our
passport country?

THOUGHTS AND FEELINGS
About moving back

The next few pages are for writing down your thoughts and feelings about moving back to your passport country. Thoughts and feelings can change from day to day, and you might want to write down some thoughts or feelings today and others another day.

THOUGHTS

Something I think about a lot:

When I think too much it helps me to:

THOUGHTS AND FEELINGS

Feelings

REMEMBER THAT FEELINGS COME AND GO AND THAT THEY CAN BE EASY OR HARD TO NOTICE. SOMETIMES FEELINGS COME ONE AT A TIME, OTHER TIMES A WHOLE BUNCH OF FEELINGS CAN COME AT ONCE. THERE ARE NO RIGHT OR WRONG FEELINGS, BUT THEY CAN BE RATHER CONFUSING AT TIMES. REMEMBER WHEN WE SHOWED YOU THE SIX MOST COMMON FEELINGS?

WHICH FEELINGS DESCRIBE WHAT YOU'RE GOING THROUGH?

(GO BACK AND HAVE A LOOK AT PAGES 20–21)

SADNESS

DISGUST

ANGER

SURPRISE

FEAR

JOY

Today

DIARY PAGES
What's on your mind?

THOUGHTS AND FEELINGS

Today

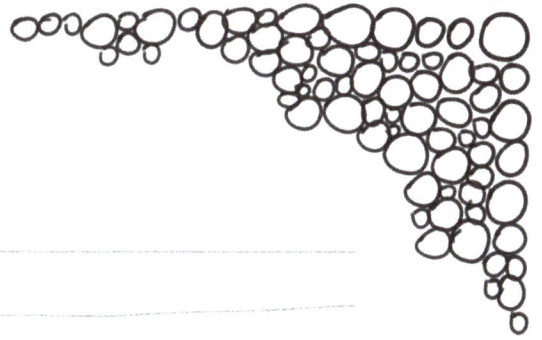

Today

THOUGHTS AND FEELINGS

Our last week before leaving _____

TIME	SUNDAY	MONDAY	TUESDAY
7am-8am			
8am-9am			
9am-10am			
10am-11am			
11am-12am			
12am-1pm			
1pm-2pm			
2pm-3pm			
3pm-4pm			
4pm-5pm			
5pm-6pm			
6pm-7pm			
7pm-8pm			
8pm-9pm			

WEDNESDAY	THURSDAY	FRIDAY	SATURDAY

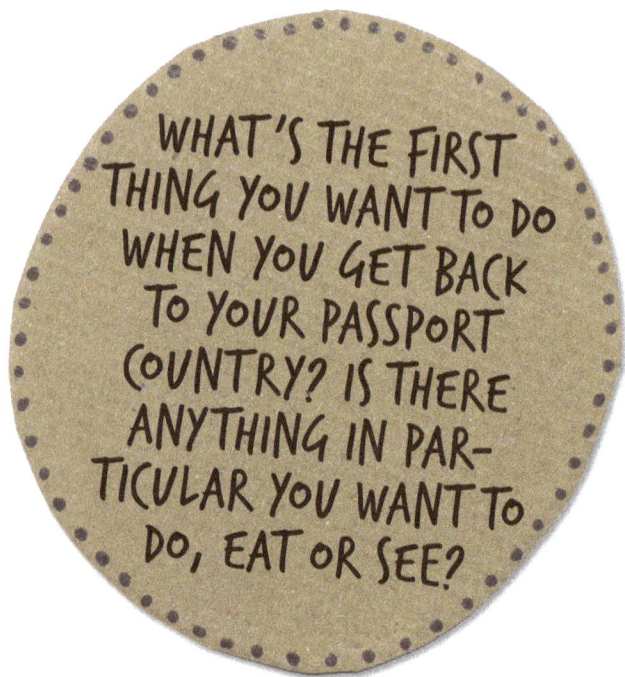

WHAT'S THE FIRST THING YOU WANT TO DO WHEN YOU GET BACK TO YOUR PASSPORT COUNTRY? IS THERE ANYTHING IN PARTICULAR YOU WANT TO DO, EAT OR SEE?

The journey back

DID ANYONE PICK YOU UP AT THE AIRPORT?

WHEN DID YOU FIRST VISIT FAMILY AND FRIENDS?

WHAT WAS THAT LIKE?

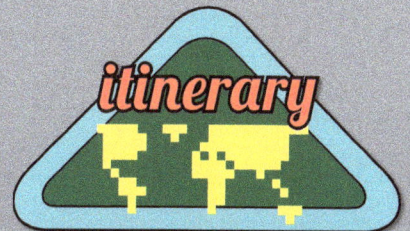

itinerary

OUR FIRST WEEK BACK IN _____

TIME	SUNDAY	MONDAY	TUESDAY
7am–8am			
8am–9am			
9am–10am			
10am–11am			
11am–12am			
12am–1pm			
1pm–2pm			
2pm–3pm			
3pm–4pm			
4pm–5pm			
5pm–6pm			
6pm–7pm			
7pm–8pm			
8pm–9pm			

WEDNESDAY	THURSDAY	FRIDAY	SATURDAY

Lots of people find that returning to their passport country after living somewhere else is like crossing a big bridge because of all the steps along the way. Maybe you have crossed lots of these steps – maybe only some of them. Perhaps you're standing on one of them right now? Maybe you've noticed other steps along the bridge that you can write down. Where are you standing right now?

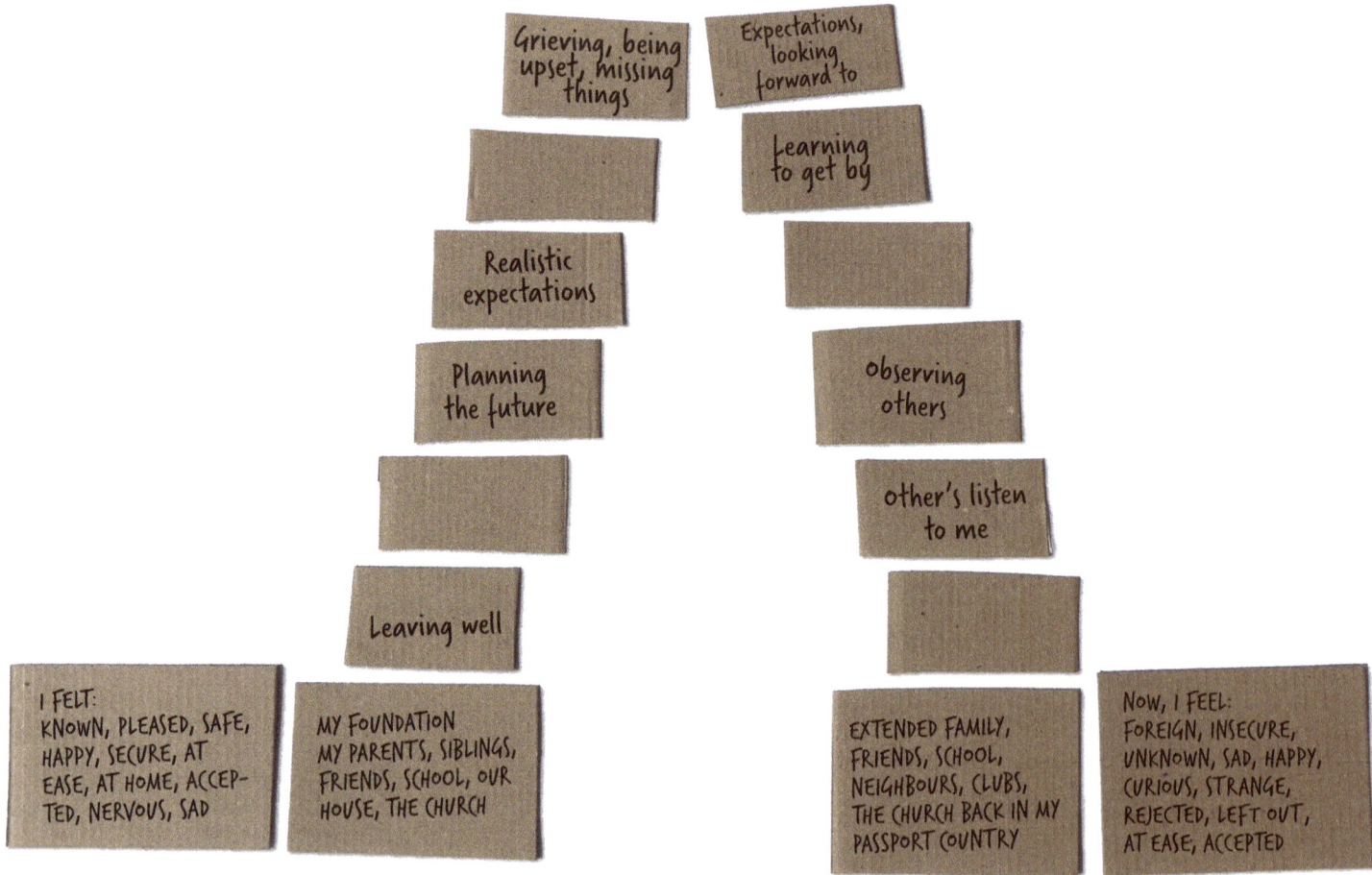

Grieving, being upset, missing things

Expectations, looking forward to

Learning to get by

Realistic expectations

Planning the future

observing others

other's listen to me

Leaving well

I FELT:
KNOWN, PLEASED, SAFE, HAPPY, SECURE, AT EASE, AT HOME, ACCEPTED, NERVOUS, SAD

MY FOUNDATION MY PARENTS, SIBLINGS, FRIENDS, SCHOOL, OUR HOUSE, THE CHURCH

EXTENDED FAMILY, FRIENDS, SCHOOL, NEIGHBOURS, CLUBS, THE CHURCH BACK IN MY PASSPORT COUNTRY

NOW, I FEEL:
FOREIGN, INSECURE, UNKNOWN, SAD, HAPPY, CURIOUS, STRANGE, REJECTED, LEFT OUT, AT EASE, ACCEPTED

FEELINGS

RE-ENTRY IS A WORD PEOPLE USE TO DESCRIBE MOVING BACK TO YOUR PASSPORT COUNTRY.

the EXPERT says

For some TCK's, re-entry feels like going home. For others it feels like moving to a whole new country that you barely know. On the next few pages we have gathered some advice about re-entry from other TCKs who have been through it!

RE-ENTRY

the TCK says

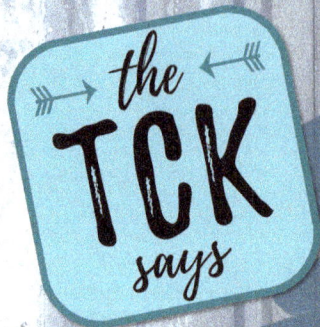

IDA'S RE-ENTRY STORY

Going back was so hard. I felt like an invisible immigrant and that I didn't fit in. My attitude was different, my clothes were different, the music I listened to was different — things that are a big deal for a teenager. My family was still in Malawi, so I didn't even have them to support me. I was glad to find others at boarding school like me. They had moved around a lot and their families were abroad, too. We were naturally drawn to one another and I felt like they understood me. All the students from my passport country found me weird because I was so different. I felt like a lot of my experiences were much harsher than theirs and eventually I stopped telling my stories because they seemed extreme compared to their 'protected lives' in a safe country. Children who move back to their passport countries after living abroad are not home. Home is no longer their passport country — at least not for me. It was tough getting my parents to realise and accept that.

Getting together with TCKs like yourself is a great support when you move back.

TCK

Other TCKs know what you're going through! Talk to them about it. It's interesting how my best friends after we got back were other TCKs or outsiders.
–Ida

It's so cool that someone recognizes some of the things I've been through.

Others feel just like me and can relate to how i feel.

You can meet other TCKs who understand you.

Let out your feelings so they don't stay inside.

People are interested, they listen, and they understand.

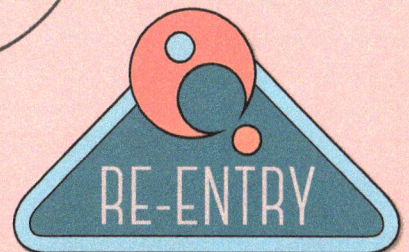

RE-ENTRY

Sometimes feeling different hurts — but remember that you're unique!

ACCEPT THAT SOME PEOPLE JUST DON'T UNDERSTAND WHAT YOU'VE EXPERIENCED BUT TRY TO EXPLAIN ANYWAY.

Save some small things from the places you have lived or been and keep them.

Who you are isn't determined by where you come from.

Good advice

Getting to know several cultures is a great advantage. You see the world in a special way!

YOU'RE NOT ALONE WITH YOUR STRUGGLES.

REACH OUT TO THOSE AROUND YOU AND SHARE YOUR THOUGHTS AND STORIES WITH THEM.

Be honest with yourself and others about what you are struggling with!

You're good enough just the way you are — you might be good at fitting in, but make sure that you're being yourself!

YOU WILL FEEL DIFFERENT – AND THAT'S OK! I EXPERIENCED CULTURE SHOCK WHEN WE MOVED BACK, EVEN THOUGH I THOUGHT I KNEW THIS COUNTRY.
– INGEBORG

I don't think everyone is going to understand. I may look just like them and behave just like them. No one can tell that I've lived abroad.
– Hannah

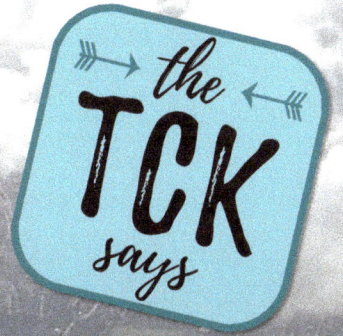

the TCK says

More good advice

I wish I had gotten some advice on how to behave in my passport country. Like – how do people make friends?
– Elisabeth

Settling in takes a long time. I don't feel at home in my own country, and I don't think I ever will. But it does get better. After a couple of years it gets better.
– Ingeborg

In Tanzania swearing is not allowed. Here, everyone swears all the time.
– Hannah

RE-ENTRY

SETTLING IN TAKES TIME AND THAT'S COMPLETELY NORMAL.
KEEPING TRACK OF HOW YOU'RE DOING EACH MONTH CAN HELP
YOU SEE IF IT GETS BETTER ALONG THE WAY.
FOR SOME PEOPLE SETTLING IN IS QUICK AND EASY — FOR
OTHERS IT CAN TAKE ONE OR TWO YEARS. BUT
IT GRADUALLY GETS BETTER. MARK THE MOOD
THAT DESCRIBES EACH MONTH.

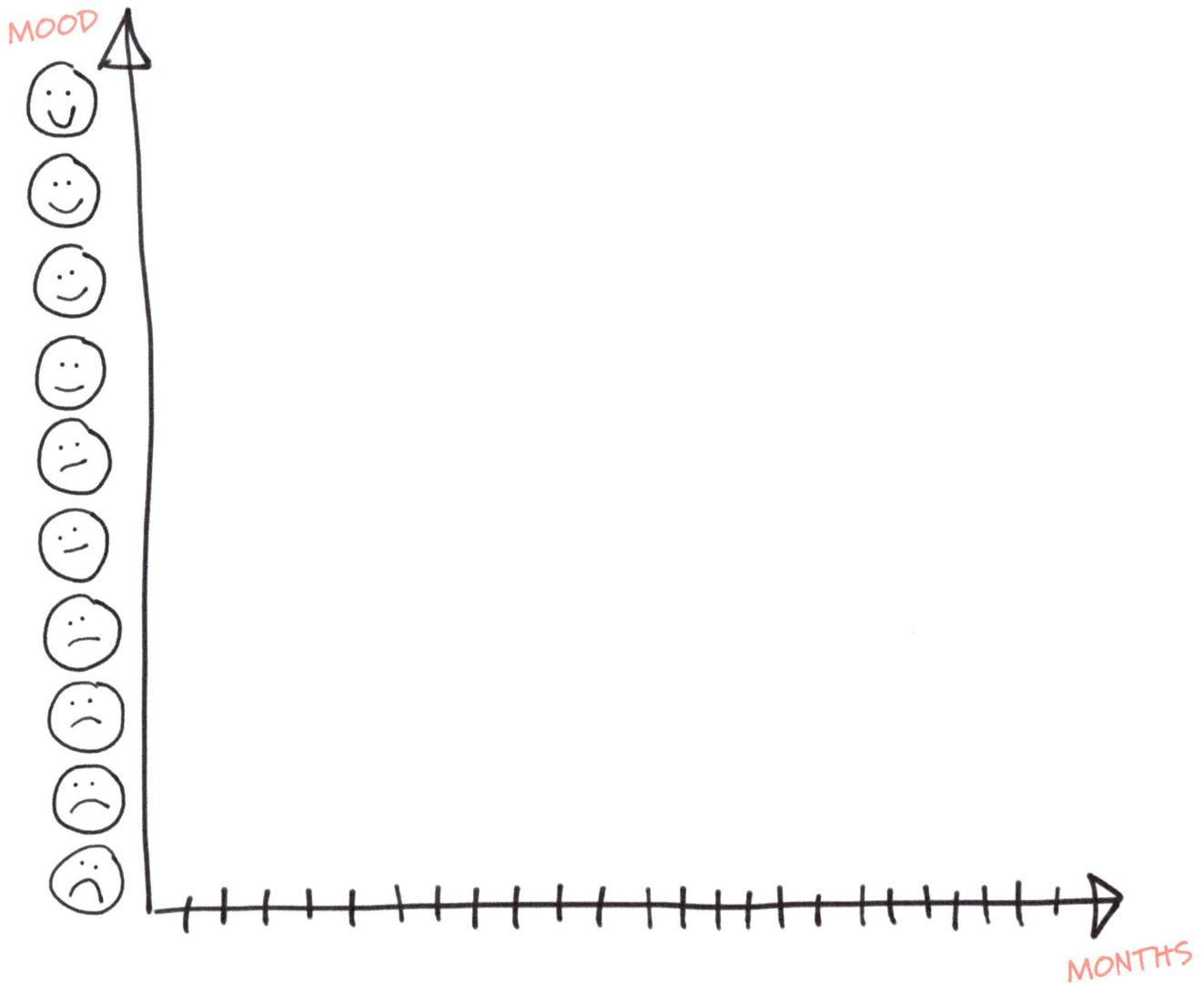

MOOD

MONTHS

Does this sound familiar?

People react differently when they move back to their passport country. Three reactions are particularly common during re-entry. Do any of them remind you of how you have reacted?

THE WALLFLOWER
Tries to stay invisible, observing everything from the side-lines.

THE CHAMELEON
Tries to blend in by acting like everyone else.

THE SCREAMER
Clearly declares being different than everyone else.

RE-ENTRY

Is your reaction different altogether? Describe or draw how you are reacting to moving back to your passport country.

What am I going back to?

HOUSE, SCHOOL,
FAMILY AND FRIENDS
HOBBIES AND ACTIVITIES

Will I be going to a new school?

Or going back to my old school from before we left?

Will the class change with me in it?

Will it change the groups and friendships?

Will those changes be for the best?

What about my old friends?

Will they have found new friends while I was away?

Will they still want to be friends with me?

NEW WAYS OF SPENDING TIME WITH FRIENDS

A lot may have changed while you've been gone.

Your friends might not really 'play' anymore — they might just

want to hang out or play games on their tablets or phones.

You may be worrying about making friends again. If you

are, go back and read pages 81-89 about making friends.

And remember: You have made new friends before,

and you will make new friends this time, too.

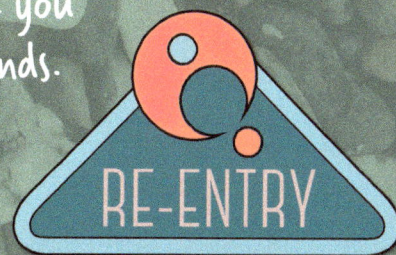

Many children spend a lot of time playing games or chatting with each other on their phones

WHAT ARE THE BENEFITS OF USING YOUR PHONE WITH YOUR FRIENDS?

WHAT ARE THE DISADVANTAGES OF USING YOUR PHONE WITH YOUR FRIENDS?

IF YOU'D PREFER THAT PHONES WEREN'T SUCH A BIG PART OF HANGING OUT, IT IS OKAY TO:

- AGREE WITH YOUR FRIENDS TO LEAVE YOUR PHONES IN THE HALLWAY UNTIL ONE OF YOU HAS TO GO HOME.

- LET YOUR PARENTS DECIDE ON SOME HOUSE RULES FOR HOW MUCH TIME YOU'RE ALLOWED TO SPEND USING YOUR PHONE IN THE HOUSE.

- AGREE WITH A FRIEND TO LIMIT THE TIME YOU SPEND ON YOUR PHONES WHEN YOU'RE SPENDING TIME TOGETHER.

It's funny how kids here get their own phones when they're 10. It makes you feel different if you're not used to it — but that's OK.
— Hannah

the EXPERT says

Remember that many children use their phones a lot. That doesn't mean that they don't want to hang out with you! Changing how you spend time with friends — like using phones less — can take time. Be patient

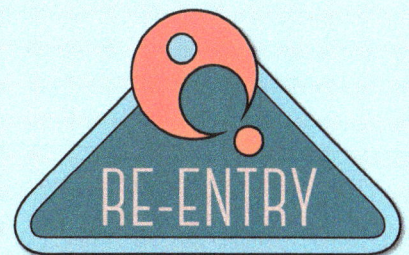

RE-ENTRY

DO YOU KNOW THE FEELING?

HERE ARE SOME QUOTES DESCRIBING SOME OF THE COMMON THOUGHTS THIRD CULTURE KIDS MAY HAVE. CAN YOU RELATE TO THEM? FEELING THIS WAY CAN BE HARD SOMETIMES, BUT IT'S VERY COMMON.

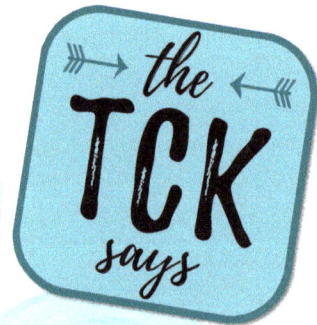

Sometimes I feel like I'm bragging when telling people regular things about my life.

the TCK says

It makes me feel all alone when I feel like I don't fit in.

I'm not like everyone else.

Sometimes I don't know where I belong.

SOME OF MY FRIENDS SEEM A LOT LESS MATURE THAN ME.

I OFTEN FEEL LIKE NO ONE AROUND ME GETS ME.

I often behave in a certain way just to try to fit in.

One of the things I've cried about the most is not knowing where I come from.

ARE YOU A LANGUAGE PRO?

AFTER LIVING ABROAD YOU'RE PROBABLY SKILLED AT SPEAKING TWO OR MORE LANGUAGES. THAT'S SO COOL! GOING BACK TO YOUR PASSPORT COUNTRY AND SPEAKING A WHOLE NEW LANGUAGE CAN BE TOUGH, BECAUSE IT MEANS THAT YOU MIGHT BE A LITTLE OUT OF PRACTICE SPEAKING YOUR MOTHER TONGUE.

THAT MEANS THAT YOU MIGHT MAKE SOME SILLY MISTAKES OR GET EXPRESSIONS ALL WRONG. HERE IS SOME SPACE TO READ SOME EMBARRASSING AND COOL STORIES AND SHARE YOUR OWN.

TCK

I spoke English fluently, but the problem was speaking my mother tongue — and writing was even worse!
– Ida

TCK

Some of the slang and the expressions sounded like something from a totally different planet to me.
– Julie

TCK

NOT LONG AFTER WE MOVED BACK I SAID AN EXPRESSION ALL WRONG IN FRONT OF THE WHOLE CLASS AND THEY ALL BURST OUT LAUGHING AT ME. IT WAS SO EMBARRASSING. BUT NOW THAT I'M OLDER, I CAN LAUGH ABOUT IT TOO.

– EMMA

TCK

When we got back from the UK, I spoke English fluently, but my classmates had only just begun English lessons. They weren't very good at it. I was embarrassed by my thick British accent, so I tried to tone it down a lot, so I wouldn't stand out too much.
– Simon

TCK

RE-ENTRY

the
TCK
says

ONE OF THE THINGS I FOUND HARD TO GET USED TO WAS THE LACK OF DISCIPLINE IN CLASS. I HAD GONE TO A STRICT INTERNATIONAL SCHOOL. BUT WHEN I GOT BACK TO MY PASSPORT COUNTRY EVERYONE WAS NOISY IN CLASS AND GOING TO SCHOOL WAS TAKEN FOR GRANTED. I HAD A HARD TIME DEALING WITH THAT.

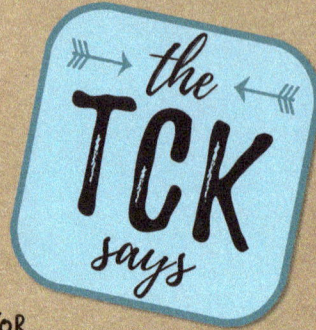

– SARAH

WRITE DOWN SOME OF THE EXPERIENCES YOU HAVE HAD SETTLING IN.

Will you still listen to me?

Maybe you will get a sense that people around you are only interested in hearing about your 'exotic life abroad' for a short period of time and then just stop asking. This can be very upsetting and make you feel like your stories and memories don't matter or that no one understands you. Some don't understand, others are busy, and others still might just want to hear it little by little. Be patient and keep on sharing your stories with the people around you!

The first few days after we got back, everyone kept asking if I had seen a lot of lions and elephants. I hadn't. They didn't seem to care about my house or my friends, and that made me feel alone.
— Jonathan

TCK

IDEAS FOR TELLING OTHERS ABOUT YOUR LIFE ABROAD:

-SHOW THEM PARTS OF THIS BOOK — LIKE THE COLLECTION PAGES.

-SHOW THEM PHOTOS OR VIDEOS YOU'VE TAKEN.

- INVITE THEM OVER FOR SOME LOCAL FOOD.

-ASK YOUR MUM OR DAD TO COME AND TELL YOUR NEW CLASSMATES ALL ABOUT LIFE IN THE COUNTRY WHERE YOU LIVED.

RE-ENTRY

Everyone has a story worth listening to

take a chance and ask someone about their story, or tell them yours

Your life abroad has taken you to special places and made you unique. But remember that everyone has their own unique story — no matter where they grew up or how much they moved. Explore what you have in common as well as what your differences are.

→→ the
EXPERT
says ←←

KEEP BEING CURIOUS ABOUT THE PEOPLE AROUND YOU, EVEN IF THEY ARE NOTHING LIKE YOU. THEY ALSO HAVE A STORY. EVEN THOUGH THEIR EXPERIENCES ARE DIFFERENT THAN YOURS, YOUR FEELINGS MIGHT BE THE SAME.

the EXPERT says

IF YOU KEEP FEELING UPSET SIX MONTHS AFTER YOU GET BACK, IT'S IMPORTANT TO TALK TO SOMEONE WHO CAN HELP YOU GET BETTER. TAKE A LOOK AT PAGE 158 AND TALK TO YOUR PARENTS ABOUT HOW TO GET BETTER AND SETTLE IN.

AFTER 3 MONTHS
—How are you doing now?

Have you started to settle in or are you still struggling to do so? It can take a long time and be really hard. Occasionally, it can make you feel like you're all alone with all the thoughts in your head. Try sharing them with someone you trust and talk to.

Settling in takes a long time. I don't feel at home in my own country, and I don't think I ever will. But it does get better. After a couple of years, it gets better.
— Ingeborg

TCK

RE-ENTRY

BIBLIOGRAPHY

Antonovsky, A. (1987): *Unravelling the Mystery of Health*. How people manage stress and stay well. Jossey Bass.

Blohm, J. (1996): *Where in the World are you going?* Intercultural Press, INC. A Nicholas Brealey Company. (P. 43 is based on p. 49-51 in Blohm, and p. 55 is based on p. 35-36 in Blohm, and p. 58-60 are based on p. 38-41 in Blohm). Reproduced by permission of Intercultural Press, an Imprint of Nicholas Brealey Publishing. Copyright © by Judith M. Blohm.

Bowlby, J. (2005) *The making and breaking of affectional bonds*. Taylor & Frances Ltd.

Bowlby, J. (1990) *A secure base – Parent-Child Attachment and Healthy Human Development*. Basic Books

Broberg, A., Granqvist, P., Ivarsson, T., Mothander, P.R (2008) *Tilknytningsteori- Betydningen af nære følelsesmæssige relationer*. Hans Reitzels Forlag

Docter, P. (2015) *Inside out* [DVD] Disney Pixar

Ekman, Paul (1999): *Basic Emotions* IN: Handbook of cognition and emotion. Edited by T. Dalgleish & M. Power. John Wiley & sons.

Høgsted, R & Berthelsen, A. (2015): *Missionen går til*. Forsvarsakademiet

Iyer, P. (2013, June). *Pico Iyer: Where is home?* [Video file]. Retrieved from https://www.ted.com/talks/pico_iyer_where_is_home

Knell, M. (2007) *Burn up or splash down*. Authentic Publishing

Knell, M. (2001) *Families on the move. Growing up overseas – and loving it!* Monarch Books. P 150 is based on p. 141 in Knell. Based on p. 140-142 by permission of the writer. Copyright 2001 by Marion Knell

Pittman, L (2012): *Expat Teen talks*. Summertime Publishing

Poon Tip, B. (2016). *Do Big small things. A guided journey toward freedom, happiness and adventure*. Running press

Pollock, D., Van Reken, R. & Pollock M. (2017) *Third culture Kids. Growing up among worlds*. 3rd edition. Nicholas Brealey Publishing. © 1999, 2001, 2009, 2017 by David C. Pollock, Michael Pollock and Ruth Van Reken. P. 157 is based on p. 75 in Pollock, Pollock & Van Reken (2017) With permission from Nicholas Brealey Publishing.

Saint-Exupéry, A (1946;2004). *The Little Prince*. Egmont Publishing. P.85-89 are quoted from Saint Exupéry

Simonsen, R.T & Prip, A. (2012). *Mit liv som delebarn*. FADL's Forlag A/S

Simonsen, R.T & Prip, A. (2012). *Mit liv som deleteenager*. FADL's Forlag A/S

Siegel, D. J (2014). *Brainstorm. The power and purpose of the teenage brain*. Penguin Publishing

Siegel, D. & Bryson, T.P (2012). *The Whole-Brain Child: 12 Revolutionary Strategies to Nurture Your Child's Developing Mind*. Random House Publishing Group

Stallard, P. (2002). T*hink Good Feel Good - A Cognitive Behavior Therapy Workbook for Children and Young People*. John Wiley & Sons

Stallard, P. (2005). *A Clinician's Guide to Think Good-feel Good - Using CBT with Children and Young People*. John Wiley & Sons

Ward, C., Bochner S. & Furnham, A. (2001) *The Psychology of Culture Shock*. Routledge,UK.

BOOKS

Besanceney, V (2014) *B at Home: Emma Moves Again*. Summertime Publishing

Bushong, Lois (2013). *Belonging everywhere and nowhere*. Mango Tree Intercultural Services, USA

Costa, S. et al. (2009). *The Mission of Detective Mike: Moving abroad* – A story to Help Expat Children Understand the Relocation process. Summertime Publishing.

Crossmann, T. (2016) *Misunderstood – The impact of growing up overseas in the 21st century*. Summertime Publishing.

Gardner, M. (2014). *Between worlds: Essays on Culture and Belonging*. Doorlight Publications

Ota, D.W. (2014) *Safe Passage* – How mobility affects people & what international school should do about it. Summertime Publishing.

Knell, M. (2007) *Burn up or splash down*. Authentic Publishing

Knell, M. (2001). *Families on the move. Growing up overseas and loving it*. Monarch Books UK

Maffini, H. (2011) *Sammy's next move* – Sammy the snail is a travelling snail who lives in different countries. Third Culture Kids Press.

Murray, T. (2013) *Hidden in my Heart: A TCKs journey through cultural transition*. Bottomline Media

Pittman, L. (2012) *Expat teens talk*. Summertime publishing

Pollock, D.,Van Reken, R. & Pollock M. (2017) *Third culture Kids. Growing up among worlds*. 3rd edition. Nicholas Brealey Publishing

Saint-Exupéry, A (1946;2004). *The Little Prince*. Egmont Publishing.

Quick, Tina. (2010) *The global Nomad's Guide to University Transition*. Summertime Publishing

Center for Family Development – Unit for expats

'Go' is created by psychologists Maria Kofod Techow, Emilie Frijs Due and Bente skovby Burke at Center for Family Development, a Danish NGO striving towards supporting well-being in families.Unit for expats is a branch of the NGO with 30 years of experience working with relocating families in various sectors. Unit for expats specializes in rendering psychological support before, during and after international postings. We provide screening, preparation sessions, children's groups and meet-ups for young TCKs. Our approach is focused on working with the whole family – not just the employee. We believe that strong relationships, knowing what to expect and how to deal with the challenges of international life are key ingredients to successful expatriation.

Interested in keeping up with our work and initiatives? Go to: www.familieudvikling.dk

Reach us at: mkt@familieudvikling.dk

CENTER FOR FAMILIEUDVIKLING
Center for Family Development

ACKNOWLEDGEMENTS

Like most books, this one is the result of a lengthy process - from the first idea to publishing the Danish version in October 2016. We are so thrilled that the Danish version has been so well received, which has resulted in the book now being published in English. Created in Denmark, parts of the book may have a nordic outlook on some issues. Our hope is that the book might help children throughout the world before, during and after expatriation to feel a sense of coherence in their lives. May the book help them deal with the challenges they face and help them to experience their lives as meaningful.

A big thank you to all the children, adolescents and adults who have shared their stories about growing up abroad and returning to their passport countries. Your stories have truly shaped this book!

Thank you to my colleagues and co-authors psychologists Emilie and Bente for your sense of humor, your wisdom, creativity, collaboration and inspiring conversations throughout this process. It has been a great pleasure creating this book together with you.

Thank you Jonas Jørgensen and Maria Hastrup from the Danish Mission Council, who were involved in the first steps towards creating the book.

Thanks to Danes Worldwide and Pia Porsborg Solmer for inspiration, ideas and for our future collaboration in using the book.

Thank you Helle Granhøj, Helle Højby and Inger Chercka for reading the book with professional eyes and sharing insight and ideas.

Thank you Judith, Johannes and Adam, for reading the book from the perspective of a child/adolescent and for sharing useful reflections.

Thank you Emilie Frijs Due and Jon Jay Neufeld, for your help translating the book into English and for your helpful insights on cultural differences, the perspective of the parents and much more.

Thank you Ida Stilling, who is an ATCK (Adult Third Culture Kid) and recently obtained a master's degree in Culture, Communication and Globalization from Aalborg University. Thank you for your many reflections, quotes and your passionate advocacy for TCKs!

A big thanks to Camilla Engrob for her beautiful visuals and illustrations. Thank you for your ability to sense what appeals to children and for your creative skills in transforming ideas into visuals. And not least, thanks for your patience through the constant flow of new ideas and edits.

Finally, a big thanks to all of the TCKs who read the book and shared their ideas, quotes, advice, poems, honesty and creativity: Elisabeth, Ludvig, Ingeborg, Hannah, Christine, Mathias, Elisabeth and Signe – you have helped write a very special book and you're all so special!

Maria Kofod Techow, co-author of the book, head of Unit for Expats and psychologist.

www.ingramcontent.com/pod-product-compliance
Lightning Source LLC
Chambersburg PA
CBHW061223270326
41927CB00024B/3477